SINGING IN
MY BLOOD

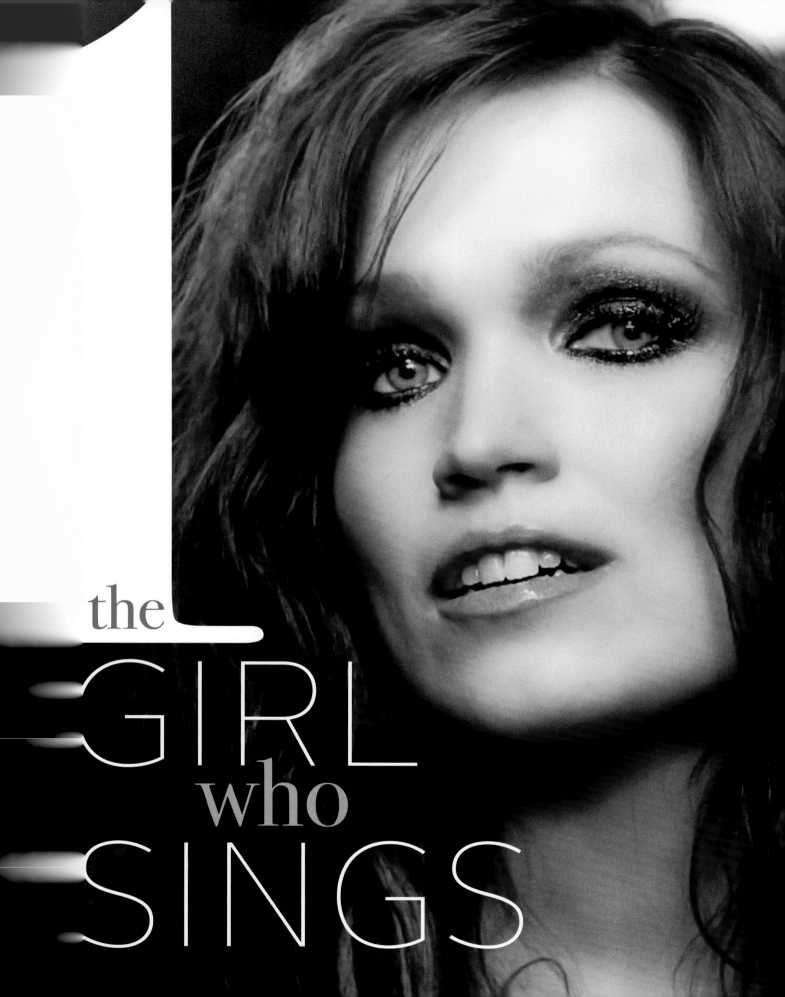

the
GIRL
who
SINGS

My story begins in Finland, in a village called Puhos, where I was born on August 17, 1977. Surrounded by forests and lakes, Puhos is about 14 kilometres from the larger town of Kitee in the region of Northern Karelia. When I was small, the main employer in Puhos was a paper factory where most of the other kids' parents worked, but my father was a carpenter who mainly built houses – we always lived in a house that he had built – and my mother was a secretary who also worked part-time as a vet in Kitee.

Puhos was not very big; it had a population of about 500 people served by two supermarkets, a bank and a post office, but I was never bored. I have two brothers – Timo, who is seven years older than me, and Toni, who is five years younger – but as a child I spent a lot of time on my own in the forest that bordered the village, collecting berries and making up stories and adventures. I would build secret hiding places under the trees, gather flowers and play with insects, and in the winter, I would play in the snow and make snow caves. It was a huge forest and I was always very aware of its hidden dangers: there were bears and foxes and sometimes I would hear moose running about. The forest was my magical place where I could be still and happy.

We were really spoiled by all the beautiful nature that surrounded us. Like a lot of Finns, we had a summer lakehouse, which was about 20 kilometres from our village. It was in the middle of nowhere and we would drive there along a sandy road. We also used to take caravan holidays and, when I was around eight or nine, we travelled to a beautiful place called Mäntyranta in Kesälahti. Although it is quite near Puhos, it's more like being on the Spanish coast. The sand is golden, with a lake so pure and clean you can see fish swimming in it. It was there that I met a girl called Sirja Tiilikainen, who was a year older than me. For a while, every

ABOVE I was around five years old in this photo and getting ready to sing on our friend's birthday. My mum made my dress.

year her parents would holiday at that same spot and we would all meet up. Even at a young age she was very into clothing and fashion and we became firm friends. She would later play a very important role in creating my stage outfits for both Nightwish and my solo career.

⁜ ——— ⁜ ——— ⁜

*W*e have always been a close family and, although we are all very different, we have always bonded over our shared love of music. Growing up, music was everywhere, even in our summer house, where we would sing by the campfire and listen to the radio or play music on our cassette player. My parents both had great singing voices although they did not play any instruments. I began learning to play the piano when I was six and for my eighth birthday they bought me my first piano. It was a Hellas upright piano – a Finnish make – and it is now my daughter's piano. I was not the only person in my family to learn an instrument, though: Timo played drums and Toni, who is very talented, can play almost any instrument. But it was Timo who introduced me to rock music. He would play Kiss, W.A.S.P., Alice Cooper and even Iron Maiden, Scorpions and Whitesnake: he was a real rocker, and I really enjoyed listening to his melodic hard-rock records. He now performs popular Finnish music under the name Teo Turunen.

Singing is in my blood. Ever since I was a little girl I have enjoyed performing in front of people.

But rock was just one type of music that I was listening to and my tastes as a kid were very different from the music I make now. I loved Bonnie Tyler, and thought she had a very unique voice, and I loved playing her *Faster Than the Speed of Night* album on vinyl. She was the first artist I went to see in concert, when I was about 11 or 12. I took a train with my friend Sirja to Helsinki, where Bonnie was performing at a festival, and she was incredible.

Maggie Reilly was another singer I really liked. I remember saving up my pocket money to buy her 1992 *Echoes* album – the first I ever bought. I had that record on repeat play and I learned all the lyrics by singing along. Another very influential artist for me was Whitney Houston – she had a voice that I adored, and I loved her first two albums, *Whitney Houston* and *Whitney*, especially the songs 'The Greatest Love of All' and 'Didn't We Almost Have It All'. Nobody else could sing like her.

Singing is in my blood. Ever since I was a little girl I have enjoyed performing
in front of people. Whenever my parents had visitors, I would put on a puppet
show for them, play the piano, or show off my wardrobe and how many dresses
I had. I loved musicals, too, and whenever my parents took me to the theatre, I
always wanted to see what was going on behind the curtain and to learn how it all
worked. In my village, people would say, "That's the girl who sings!" and I would
be asked to sing at weddings and local village events. My first public performance
was when I was around six or seven and I sang a solo in our community centre.
It was a very popular venue where everybody in the village would gather for
birthdays and parties; bands would play there at the weekends and people
would go there to dance. I can remember standing in front of the audience and
being so frightened that I forgot the lyrics. I can't remember what I sang, but I do
remember it being a terrifying experience!

Early in primary school, I joined the school choir and loved it. I enjoyed
getting together with a big group of singers and rehearsing for performances.
Although everyone in my family was musical, I was the only one who really studied
classical music and, five times a week, my parents would take me to different
lessons in the evenings. In addition to the choir, I learned flute, piano, music
history and theory and, by the time I was 13 or 14 years old, I decided I wanted to
be a professional singer.

> It was amazing how my **confidence** grew in that time. I could look myself in the mirror and know that I was OK, that I was **not crazy.**

In Finland, kids start school at seven, and I went to the local primary until I was about 13. I was very badly bullied and so hated school. I did not want to go, to the point that it made me ill, and music became my haven. I would go to my room and play the piano and sing to escape. I had my forest, my brothers and my friends, but at school, the girls were very mean to me.

The school headmaster was himself a musician, and he thought I had some talent and supported me. That was reason enough for some of the girls in the year above to see me as the teacher's pet, which was not cool. When I reached my final year of primary school in Puhos, they had all moved on to the last three primary years in Kitee school, and I felt reborn because nobody was bullying or teasing me. It was amazing how my confidence grew in that time. I could look myself in the mirror and know that I was OK, that I was not crazy. When I turned 13 and moved to that same school in Kitee to complete my primary education, I was scared to face the bullies again, but they were ashamed of what they had done – to the extent that one of them even came to apologise. That was an amazing moment.

Around this time, the school music teacher, Plamen Dimov, encouraged me to focus more on singing. He wanted me to become another Whitney Houston; I was performing her songs at school, but I started to have problems with my voice. They are difficult songs and I was getting a sore throat from singing them because I could not deliver the high notes. I was about 14 and I got scared. I said to my teacher, "I don't like this. I have to get help." He adored me but he was not a vocal coach and so couldn't help. Even in Kitee there were not many singing teachers, but we found one who took me on as a private student and started to train me as a classical, lyrical singer. I was about 15 by that time, and it was mind-blowingly different from what I had thought. Although I had learned about the history of classical music at school and had a cassette collection of classical music that I'd bought with my pocket money, classical singing was completely new to me. My voice changed radically over the course of a few weeks. It was a fantastic adventure and made me want to learn everything I could about singing.

When I was about 14 or 15 years old, I performed in my first proper concert as a soloist, at Kitee Church. Being a Lutheran church, it is quite plain but is spread across two floors and is built of red and grey stone with a very tall steeple.

Sirja Tiilikainen, dressmaker

"Tarja and I used to spend our childhood summers on a campsite called Mäntyranta in Kesälahti. It's a beautiful place with a long beach and amazing clear waters. There was always so much to do, such as swimming and playing games together. There were usually a lot of other kids there, so we would often play hide-and-seek with them. We always looked forward to the summer because that was when we got to spend loads of time together.

"I remember one year we both turned up in the same black-and-yellow-striped dress. We had ordered them independently of each other through a mail-order catalogue and it was such a surprise when we realised what we'd done. I still have a photo of us in our matching dresses. In another photo, I can see that we had a great idea of smudging coal onto our faces, but luckily we do our makeup better nowadays!

"A few years ago, I had the chance to travel with Tarja and her band in Europe for almost two weeks. I had such a great time, everyone was lovely and I got to see what happens behind the scenes. It was so nice to be a part of that 'family' for a brief moment. All of her concerts are special, of course,

but it was fabulous to see that her audience includes everyone from young goths to retired old bikers. I love that her music moves all kinds of people.

"Before the tour, Tarja and her band were rehearsing, but I mostly sat in a hotel room sewing her stage outfits which I had brought with me. Marcelo managed to borrow a very old sewing machine for me to work with, which didn't always work properly, but I still managed to get everything made with it.

"The last evening I was with them was in Hamburg, so a few of the crew and I went out for drinks. We ended up in the red-light district and I had a really great night taking in all the sights!

"Another funny memory is from when I was with them on the tourbus. Kevin [Chown], who then played the bass in the band, has Swedish blood, so we played Abba most of the night and sang along. I've had to apologise for my 'singing' so many times since as I really can't sing – even if my life depended on it!

"On another occasion, I was visiting Tarja in Buenos Aires and she had a meet-and-greet with her Argentinian

fan club, so I went along. One of her fans had got a dressmaker to create an exact copy of the black-and-blue coat that Tarja wears in the 'Die Alive' video, but for a Barbie doll. I thought that was so sweet. That's when I realised just how much attention her fans pay to her outfits and how much they really love them. It felt great to know that I had made dresses that were so adored.

"I've been making her stage clothing for a quite a while, so I know the sorts of things she likes. Tarja tends to tell me what she wants and then I visit a fabric store. I get my best ideas when I find the right fabric. In my workshop, I have an adjustable dressform, or mannequin, which I adjust to Tarja's exact measurements which helps a lot – especially as we're now in different countries. I use a toile, or a test pattern, made to her exact measurements as the base and build on that. Of course, every outfit will need to be fitted on her at some point, but before then we exchange a lot of pictures via email and phone.

"My absolute favourite outfit was the 'Ice Queen' dress from the cover of *My Winter Storm*. I love the finished photos of it – Tarja looks so beautiful and Heidi's makeup is just so perfect.

ABOVE Sirja came to visit me in Buenos Aires and, during my press conference, I was given a doll that was wearing a mini replica of the dress Sirja had made me for the 'Die Alive' video. She was thrilled that fans were paying tribute to her work.

The fabric used on the hood was something that Tarja and Marcelo had found, and I chose the other materials to complement it. It wasn't a difficult dress to make but, as always, the fitting was the most challenging part. It's my number one because it accompanied her first proper solo album and that meant we could start from scratch and do something completely different from the outfits she had worn in Nightwish."

My friend Janne, who played piano and organ, accompanied me. First we performed on the balcony with the organ and then we did a few songs at the front. The local priest, Sakari, who had a magnificent baritone voice, joined me for some songs. It was a low-key church concert, but it felt amazing because all these people had come to see me. My voice had changed from that Whitney Houston try-out to this very light, small, soprano voice. It was such a dream come true for a little girl like me and I remember thinking, "Wow, this is fantastic! I want to repeat this immediately."

Many years later, on December 31, 2002, I was married to my husband Marcelo by the same priest in this very same church. It was so beautiful to return there as an adult, and those memories came flooding back to me.

I wanted to learn everything I could about music, but I knew there was no future for me to study music in Puhos – I had to get away. My ultimate dream was to attend the Sibelius Academy – the only music university in Finland. First, I planned to attend Savonlinna's Senior Secondary School of Art and Music to pass the exams I needed to get into university. I worked a series of summer jobs to save money so I could study there. For a while I worked in the paper factory's canteen, washing dishes, cleaning the tables and helping the cooks. Another summer, I worked in a little coffee shop and would ride my bike there every morning to open up and bake the pastries and put the coffee on for the customers. I was very young, but I used the money I had saved so I could move to Savonlinna for my studies. At 16, I rented an apartment where my friend and I could live. I was becoming a woman but I was also having regular arguments with my father, who was not happy that at such a young age his only daughter had gone away and was also having boyfriends.

ABOVE Performing on my own for the first time at around 14 years old – with our family friend Janne Piipponen on the piano. I was so excited that people from my home town came to hear me sing.

RIGHT My first photo with Marcelo in Panama (2000) before our story began.

BELOW Our wedding day, July 26, 2003, outside the church in Kitee where I had first performed as a teenager.

The biggest sacrifice I have made in my life is being away from my family. While in Savonlinna, I was only able to see my parents every two weeks. Although we argued, they were always very supportive, especially where music was concerned. They made a lot of sacrifices for me and never said, "Don't you want to choose another profession?" Never. I had great grades at school, and I could have chosen differently but for me it was not an option. I only wanted to do music.

Studying in Savonlinna, which is just over an hour away from Puhos and very different from my tiny home village, was an amazing experience. The Senior Secondary School of Art and Music is very prestigious and one of only two secondary schools in the city but, as its name suggests, it is the only one to specialise in music and fine arts.

At times, studying there felt like being in the American TV show *Fame*. We performed a lot, and every day was very full-on – almost 24-hour entertainment. There was so much going on. With the high-school band we revisited hits from the 60s right through to the 90s, and of course studied theory and played a lot of classical music. I once played the role of Juliet in a musical version of *Romeo and Juliet* in front of a theatre audience, and looking out at the crowd was an amazing new experience. A cassette tape, and eventually a CD, of the performance was created and, even though it was a small, school release, those recordings became my first commercially available performance. At the time, however, I was very nervous and extremely critical of my singing. Things are different now, but it has taken me many years to forgive myself for mistakes I made in the past as a performer. I used to be really hard on myself, which is no doubt connected to the bullying I endured at school which dented my self-confidence.

BELOW At 17, I gave my first classical performance as a soloist in front of the choir and chamber orchestra.

While living in Savonlinna my music tastes started to broaden. I was listening to Sting, Enya, Genesis and Peter Gabriel, as well as the harder rock of Bon Jovi, the Scorpions and Metallica's *Black Album*. I also became very interested in Sarah Brightman's work. I listened to the *Phantom of The Opera* (1987) soundtrack a lot and wondered how she could sing those high notes so well. I was interested in her technique and learned how to hit those high notes in a healthy way with Arja Nikula, my classical singing school teacher at the time, who was able to get the best out of me. I was also influenced by respected Finnish classical singers such as Karita Mattila and Soile Isokoski, whose techniques I wanted to learn more about.

During those years, I had my first European tour as a soloist with the school choir, and I performed a classical concert with an orchestra in Savonlinna

Church. But one of my biggest eye-opening moments came in my first summer in Savonlinna. Every year, the city plays host to the Savonlinna Opera Festival, which is held in a beautiful medieval castle called Olavinlinna. It was to become an important event in my life. When I was 16, I volunteered to work there and got to see all the operas for free. At the time I was dreaming about becoming part of that world and, two years later, I applied for the opera choir and got in – even though my high-school singing teacher told me not to do it because my voice was not yet ready. I was the youngest singer in the opera choir. As I sang I could hear her words in my head and followed her advice by being very careful. Since then, I have returned to that same opera festival on a few occasions to perform as a soloist.

Going to that school until I was 18 gave me the skills and confidence I needed to get into Sibelius Academy, although no school can ever really prepare you for the real world. I was the first student in the school to pass with 'Excellence' in my singing exams and I remember Arja crying because she hadn't felt properly respected by her colleagues until that point. I saw her confidence growing in front of me as they realised that she knew her stuff. We are still in touch from time to time, even now. In fact, I have stayed in touch with most of my teachers, even though, after all these years, my career has turned out to be nothing like I or they expected. If you can imagine me as that young girl who so wanted to become a classical singer and then suddenly – boom! I am now in a very different field. The whole world opened up to me after I co-founded a metal band and I saw the world through different eyes. But even when I was embarking on my rock career with Nightwish while at the same time continuing my classical music studies, my old teachers were always very supportive. They were my driving force and I could always go back to them with problems or issues about singing without worrying that they did not respect me or like what I was doing with this heavy metal band. They had trust in me, and I have always had a really great relationship with my teachers.

I always knew that it takes a lot of dedication and many hours of practice to become a professional classical singer. But who could have imagined that this little girl with a big dream from a village of 500 would end up singing for millions?

TOP When I was young, my dream was to sing at Savonlinna's Olavinlinna castle one day. It felt like a milestone when I stood on its stage for the first time at just 18 years old.

ABOVE Verdi's opera *La Forza del Destino* at Savonlinna Opera Festival. I was part of the opera choir, playing a peasant.

2
one angel's
DREAM

ABOVE I took part in a production
of the modern ballet *Evangelicum*
as the only solo singer and this was
my butterfly outfit. It was really weird
walking around with these feather
butterflies suspended from wires
around my neck.

C hristmas is very important to us Finns: it is a time of year that is full of magical traditions. Our homes are decorated with flickering candles and filled with the scent of cinnamon, clementines, apples and freshly baked piparkakut – gingerbread cookies. We always had a real Christmas tree in the living room and my mother used to change our curtains to red ones in preparation for this special time.

Finns eat around the clock at Christmas and have a big feast on December 24 with baked ham, moose meat and lots of vegetable casseroles. We drink glögi, which is a glühwein, or hot spiced wine with a delicious, cinnamon taste. It is also traditional to watch the animated film *The Snowman* (1982) on TV; every child knows it and Howard Blake's song 'Walking in the Air', most famously sung by the young Welsh soprano Aled Jones. Another highlight for children is gathering around the TV to watch the moment when Santa Claus and his reindeer leave their home in Lapland to begin delivering presents. We also always pray for the snow to arrive. If there is no snow in Finland at Christmas, it is a complete catastrophe!

My most cherished memories of Christmas are of time spent with my family. We would go to local Christmas concerts and, very early on Christmas morning, to church to sing and pray. Many artists hold Christmas concerts, so the venues are filled with music and it is a tradition for families to see at least one Christmas concert every year. But we Finns are melancholic people, so our radio stations play solemn Christmas music along with the usual, well-known commercial songs.

I had always enjoyed singing Christmas songs with my friends and family, so I really wanted to release a Christmas record. In 2003 I began talking to Spinefarm Records, the heavy metal label that Nightwish were then signed to, about starting my own solo career so I could pursue other musical styles. They were very keen on the idea and we agreed that I was doing enough heavy metal with the band. I suggested doing a Christmas album and they immediately embraced the project.

However that same year, before I had even begun recording any songs, the meaning of Christmas forever changed for me. Almost two months before December 25, my mother passed away. It was a great loss and I felt I needed to make the record for her as much as for myself. After her passing, Christmas never felt the same again, but music – my therapy – helped me through that difficult time.

The single 'Yhden Enkelin Unelma' ('One Angel's Dream') was released in 2004. The title was a reference to my mother. At the time, I hoped the single would eventually lead to me performing at my own Christmas concert, but I had no idea that it would become such a huge annual tradition.

I chose two Finnish songs for the single: 'En Etsi Valtaa, Loistoa' by Jean Sibelius and 'Kun Joulu On' by Otto Kotilainen. I had sung both with my family, my friends, and even in church, when I was a kid. They are very traditional songs that need to be sung well and, as I have always liked a challenge, I wanted to see if I was capable of that. I wanted to respect the songs and create my own acoustic, rather than classical, versions.

I was **freaking out** and climbing the walls because my voice didn't sound **natural through** the headphones ... now when I listen to it, I hear a **sweet, young voice** singing that song.

Sibelius is a very important composer in Finland; he is our musical father and the face and sound of classical Finnish music. Most Finns have been influenced by him, even metal musicians. I would love to make a record purely of Sibelius' work one day. Even though I have not lived in Finland for almost 20 years, his music still has a profound effect on me. Several years ago, a TV production team played me Sibelius' tone poem 'Finlandia' to get my reaction and I could not stop myself; I started to cry like crazy. It was so powerful, the whole experience of having to leave my home country came back in that moment. There is really no other composer that compares to Sibelius. I have sung a lot of his vocal works and they are very demanding, but it was important that one of his songs was on my first single.

Even though I had a heavy metal background, I was a classical singer and everybody had doubts about how this was going to work. Both the label and I agreed that it was very risky to make heavy metal versions of two very traditional Finnish songs. I didn't want to do that; Sibelius is so revered that you have to be careful what you do with his music. Spinefarm introduced me to the producer Esa Nieminen, who is a very famous and highly respected songwriter and TV personality in Finland. I was very excited to meet him and to learn how to work with a producer, because I had no previous experience of that and did not know what to expect. He put the team of musicians together with me and booked the studio for the recording session.

Although I was really looking forward to releasing my first solo songs, it turned into a tough recording in many ways. We recorded it in Finnvox Studios in Finland, where I had recorded the majority of Nightwish's albums, so I was very familiar with the staff and the setup, but on the day of the recording I was really sick with flu so my voice was not as it should have been. 'En Etsi Valtaa, Loistoa' has to be perfect and I was very nervous. I was under a lot of pressure and found the environment quite difficult. Nightwish had a very different sound and I had been used to recording their songs with headphones on, but I had always performed classical songs live in a large space where I could hear my natural voice. But everything was dampened down in the vocal booth; there were no vibrations, no delay or reverb: it sounded dead to me. I was freaking out and climbing the walls because my voice didn't sound natural through the headphones. I did the best I could, though, and now when I listen to it, I hear a sweet, young voice singing that song. It's also interesting that at that stage I already had full control of my voice even though I was unwell. I was also lucky to have the recording engineer Jetro Vainio supporting me. He has great hearing and would tell me, "You can do it better." He would give me very good feedback. I feel very connected to him and he has been a key production person ever since.

Jetro Vainio, recording engineer

"I first worked with Tarja on *Henkäys Ikuisuudesta*, as I was doing a lot of engineering with producer Esa Nieminen at that time. I knew Nightwish's music, of course, and I remember thinking what a huge contrast this album was, but it turned out really great. One memory that really sticks with me is of a Christmas tree and other festive decorations in the studio, which was hilarious as we recorded the vocals during the summer. After that album, Tarja's musical style got heavier again.

"The way we work together has changed a fair bit over the years. Those first albums were recorded in studios, but now we work remotely and that's actually made some things easier. For instance, it's much better to use your own recording gear that you know and love, rather than having to rely on equipment provided by a studio that you've never used before. Although there are limitations, like when musicians record their own instruments remotely, that can make things harder. Patching all the performances together is normally more challenging and complicated than it would be if the musicians were in a studio together.

"I particularly remember having a great time working at the Petrax Studio in Finland for *What Lies Beneath*. It's a residential studio so you sleep in the same building as you work. There was a sauna where we could relax with a few beers after our long days. The rest of the band was so nice and it was fun staying in such a remote area with musicians that had never even been to Finland before. It can be amazing to work in wild locations, but I don't enjoy the travelling so much any more. Although, back then I really did enjoy it all, and that period is definitely among my favourites.

"My favorite Tarja song is 'Dark Star' from *What Lies Beneath*. I remember patching the sample for the intro from pieces in the studio; it has a nice, strong guitar riff. A good, simple, melodic pop song will always get my attention.

"I always enjoy working with Tarja because the process is so well-organised and well-planned. Not every artist works in that way, but she and her team do it perfectly. And Tarja also stands out because she's become a friend. Which is good, because recording vocals with someone can be a very intimate process as you spend so much time together."

That recording session was a valuable learning process for me. If I was recording those songs now, there are many things I would do differently. I have a lot more knowledge and experience than I did then, but the record reflected who I was at that moment in time and served me very well for what was to come next.

We made two versions of each song. The first was an acoustic one with real instruments – guitar, strings, piano, flute – while on the second version we used some light programming. As Spinefarm are a heavy metal label, the boss did not think it was a good idea to put that logo on the records, so everything related to this project came out through the sublabel Passion – the name was my idea – in Finland.

Speaking of names, mine is pronounced differently according to which country you're in. 'Yhden Enkelin Unelma' was released as being simply by 'Tarja' because it is complicated enough without adding my surname. In English-speaking countries, I'm 'Tar-ja'; in Spanish-speaking countries, I'm 'Tar-ha'; in others, there are different pronunciations. (At one point, when I was on rock tours, I was thinking about printing out T-shirts with my name and the correct pronunciation under it!)

We released another variation in Argentina containing both versions of each song from the single, with the English title, 'One Angel's Dream', but still sung in Finnish. This came about because my husband has a record label, NEMS Enterprises, in Argentina, and I had a strong connection to the country even before I moved there. We also designed two different covers for the single. Even now, if I go to Finland in December, I often hear both versions of the single being played on the radio.

ABOVE I have become an emoji! Called The Voice, it depicts the idea of heavily classic, as I encapsulate Finland's two strengths: classical music and heavy metal. Finland is the first country in the world to publish its own set of 56 tongue-in-cheek emojis, which convey Finnish emotions, words and customs.

> ❝
> # If I was recording those songs now, there are many things I would do differently.

Despite the difficulties I had recording it, 'Yhden Enkelin Unelma' reached the top of the Finnish charts and I received a gold disc for it in Finland – my first – which was amazing. Soon afterwards, I got a platinum disc for it, too, which is rare for a single. I have both awards hanging on my studio wall. Of course, I wished that my mother had been there to witness that, and still feel this way today.

After the single, it was another two years before we released the Christmas album. We had agreed this with the record company so that it did not overlap with the Nightwish album scheduled for 2005 and a busy touring season with them.

It was enormously gratifying to have that kind of reception and to hear the radio playing my songs. It was very exciting, especially as the success of the single gave me the chance to tour in Finland, Germany, Spain and Romania at the end of 2005.

That tour turned into a very poignant experience because just two months before it was due to begin, in October 2005, I was fired from Nightwish. I left Finland for Buenos Aires a few days later, because I simply could not stay there. I was getting too much attention from the press, with journalists on the hunt for some gossip.

I came back to Finland for the tour that December not knowing what to expect as I had been crucified by the press who had recently printed, without even doing any proper checks, various unfounded lies about my husband and me. I didn't know whether people would come to see me or not, but it turned out to be very successful. It was comforting that I was able to bring joy to others at such a special time, just as I had experienced at Christmas concerts when I was a child. Every night there was a different audience. When I was crying onstage, I saw some of the audience weeping, too. I felt their love, which was very important because it gave me light and hope that I might be able to make it as a solo act.

ABOVE If you ever visit Buenos Aires, you can't miss its most famous monument – The Obelisk of Buenos Aires. I have a photo of it hanging on my wall at home as a reminder of the wonderful years I spent in the city.

LEFT I was very happy to have Elize Ryd from the band Amaranthe and Charlotte Wessels (ex-Delain) rocking with me in Luna Park Stadium in Buenos Aires.

I was super-excited to be onstage alone. I have always loved challenges and wanted to test myself to see if I was capable of doing it. I had been having doubts about whether just my voice and this beautiful music which had not been written by me would be enough. But it was, and it still is. I am a very sensitive person, and it was very tough at times, but I loved every minute. It was not how I had expected to launch my solo career – it started with a bang and I was thrown in at the deep end with music I had not thought I would be performing – but I've never looked back.

*W*hen it came to recording the album, *Henkäys Ikuisuudesta* (Breath From Heaven), 'Yhden Enkelin Unelma' gave it a direction. I never planned to make a radio-friendly Christmas record and I certainly didn't want to do a jolly, 'Jingle Bells' kind of album. Since my mother passed away, Christmas is no longer a happy celebration for me, and I wanted the music to make those who are lonely at this time of year feel better. And this was a theme I continued to explore on *From Spirits and Ghosts* a decade later.

I wanted to record songs that reflected my classical background, so I included Schubert's 'Ave Maria' and Bach's 'Magnificat: Quia Respexit'; they are songs I knew well and I wanted to see if I was capable of doing them justice. I also researched other Christmas songs with my husband such as 'The Eyes of a Child', which was originally released by the Australian rock duo Air Supply, 'Happy Xmas (War Is Over)' by John Lennon and 'Happy New Year' by Abba (who authorised the version I recorded which combined their English and Spanish versions).

As a newly solo artist, I also wanted to find out if I could write original music on my own. I had not written any with Nightwish and so had my first taste of songwriting on 'Kuin Henkäys Ikuisuutta', a song written by Esa that was sitting in his archive. Although it was pretty much done, I asked if I could work on it, and have a free hand in changing some of the melodies and lyrics. It felt like a good way to scratch my songwriting itch. Once I'd begun, I was hooked. I was very nervous about showing my work to professional songwriters, but you have to start somewhere, if only to gain confidence. Not everybody is able to write songs and the biggest issue for me in songwriting has always been my education: I had studied and learned so much over the years that it had boxed me in because I did not know how to be free in songwriting. I thought there were rules – but there are none. It took me many years to learn that you cannot make mistakes: if it feels right for you then that's all that matters.

We recorded *Henkäys Ikuisuudesta* (Breath From Heaven) during the summer of 2006. I put up Christmas decorations and some photographs to get me in the right mood, and even wore a Santa hat. But it was really hot in the studio and 30 degrees outside – so I was sweating while singing Christmas songs.

During those first album recordings, I began to feel more relaxed than I had when we had made the single and for Schubert's 'Ave Maria', I introduced the pianist Sonja Fräki. Sonja is Finnish and we'd met at the University of Music, Karlsruhe, Germany, where I studied between 2000 and 2002. I knew I could trust her, and when you perform *lied* – a German form of recital singing – it is a duet between pianist and singer so it is very important that it is pitch-perfect. There has to be trust and understanding between both performers. I had no reason to be nervous with Sonja; I knew she would give me confidence and support. I also brought in the flautist Emilia Kauppinen, who plays on 'Magnificat: Quia Respexit', while the rest of the musicians were introduced by Esa.

It was a very exciting project because some songs needed to be sung in a very classical style – even though I did not want the production to be 'classical'. I wanted it to be a little lighter, while at the same time treating the material with respect. We played with the sound of the piano during production so it didn't feel like a 'proper' classical recording. I wanted to tie it into the other songs and make sure that the piano didn't jar, so we tried to match the sound of John Lennon's famous white 'Imagine' piano.

Esa is very understanding and it was a very good experience working with him as a producer. He is very skilled and could spot how to do what he thought best with the vocal arrangements. Although he was not able to help me with my singing technique – I was on my own with that – he handled production perfectly.

Also on the album is a new version of 'Walking in the Air', which I included because I had performed it with Nightwish very early on in our career. Thanks to its extensive radio play in Finland, it became almost as much associated with my voice as it is with *The Snowman*. You can only guess how delighted I was when in December 2017 I got to perform it on a TV show called *SuomiLOVE* with the

ABOVE It was fun recording a Christmas album in the middle of summer! Here, you can see producer Esa Nieminen (second photo from the right, seated holding papers) and engineer Jetro Vainio (both central photos, seated at the keyboard).

OPPOSITE TOP 'Walking in the Air' from the cartoon *The Snowman* has become an important part of my yearly Christmas Concerts setlist. Here I am with Aled Jones when we sang it together.

OPPOSITE BOTTOM This concert in 2017 was a collaboration with the Finnish Embassy in Argentina to celebrate the centenary of Finland's independence from Sweden.

no-longer-a-boy-soprano Aled Jones himself. We wanted to share our love for 'Walking in the Air' with people who had gone through a difficult time in their lives, and as we sang, I thought how I'd never imagined that after recording and performing that song so many times, I would get to perform it with him. It meant such a lot to me.

The first single cut from the album, 'You Would Have Loved This', was released in October 2006, a month before the album. A music publisher had sent a selection of songs to my husband from which he picked this Cori Connors song and said, "Tarja, you should give this a listen. See what you think." When I read the lyrics I realised that it could be about my mum and that it would be a really nice piece to do. It is a very emotional song because every time I sing it, I think of her, and my listeners know this because I have made it very clear that it is dedicated to her. Everybody in the audience can relate to that and has their own stories. It is a moment in my concerts when I really have to bite my lip hard so I can deliver the song in one piece.

The album was very successful and had an amazing response from the Finnish audience. It was a Finnish record made for Finnish people, by me, a fellow Finn. On the first day of the album's release, I got a call from the record company to tell me that it had already achieved gold status in Finland. That same year, in Finland, all the local radio stations proclaimed it the Christmas Album of the Year. Since then *Henkäys Ikuisuudesta* has gone triple platinum.

A few years later, in November 2010, Universal Music (which had acquired Spinefarm Records) decided to release a special edition – *Jouluinen Platinapainos* – to celebrate the platinum sales status of the album in Finland. At the same time it was agreed that the album, originally available only in Finland and Argentina, was going to be added to all the streaming platforms and shared worldwide. I wanted to give it a new sound and make it even more Finnish. The international songs were removed and we brought in some more traditional tunes: 'Heinillä Härkien', 'Arkihuolesi Kaikki Heitä' and 'Maa On Niin Kaunis', which I had already recorded in a more acoustic style for another Christmas project. The finished album was remastered to sound more classical and more organic; it brought warmth to the mix and gave it a new lease of life.

It is now an annual tradition of mine to tour every Christmas. Even in December 2020, when concert halls were closed due to the pandemic, I performed two special Christmas Together shows that were live-streamed worldwide. But in 2006 the release of *Henkäys Ikuisuudesta* meant that my tour was larger than usual. One of the concerts was at Sibelius Hall in Lahti and on Christmas Eve it was broadcast on national TV. It was such an important moment for me.

The enthusiastic reception for *Henkäys Ikuisuudesta* helped me believe that I had a future as a solo artist, which was truly a pivotal moment. The album also set the darker tone for the music that would eventually follow. While I was working on it, I was already thinking about releasing my own solo rock records and some labels had approached me. On the threshold of a new solo career, it was a lot of work to find people who would support me and my vision, but finding a manager was one thing I didn't need to worry about – as I was already married to one.

My husband Marcelo and I first met in Chile in June 2000 during Nightwish's first South American shows. He was the band's agent there and it was during that tour that we fell in love. We spent a lot of time together just hanging out and chatting about life and our interests. I thought he was cute and enjoyed our chats but I wouldn't say it was love at first sight. He admitted that his Brazilian business partners had told him to pay me some attention because I was always

THIS SPREAD A few lineups from my Christmas concerts.

left alone with nobody to take care of me. I've always been a girl in a boys' world and it felt really nice to have a man treating me like a woman for the first time in my life.

After our first date in Panama, he told me that I was the one for him. I thought he was crazy and I literally ran away! I had been in relationships before but it had never felt like this; it was something extraordinary. I was 22 at the time, nearly 23, and had never expected to find love on the other side of the world but it happened. I remember when the band flew out of Mexico City Airport, I just collapsed because I didn't know if I would ever see Marcelo again, but he made a surprise visit to see me in Finland a few weeks later.

Marcelo has supported me from the beginning of my solo career and it's been a blessing that we've been able to work together. We're a great team and our relationship has got even better over the years. I wouldn't be where I am now without him.

I am so glad that I listened to my heart.

Film-score composer and record producer Hans Zimmer hangs his gold discs in his bathroom. Did you know that? I have adored Hans Zimmer's work for such a long time. My vision for my first solo rock album, *My Winter Storm*, was for it to have a cinematic sound, so it was a dream come true to mix the record in Zimmer's Remote Control Productions studios in California. Zimmer composed the soundtrack to so many big movies – *Gladiator*, *The Da Vinci Code*, *Pirates of the Caribbean*, you name it – he has been such a big influence on me and I really wanted him to be involved. Although I didn't work directly with him, he gave me his blessing to use his studios and I got to team up with a lot of super-talented people while I was there, including musicians, engineers, composers and sound designers who are still working with me now. One of them was Jim Dooley, who I would later make a full-length Christmas album with. Another was cellist Martin Tillman, who told me that he would be playing on the soundtrack of the next Batman movie, *The Dark Knight* (2008) – and sure enough, when I watched the film I could hear his creepy cello on it. I remember weeping in the studio in Zurich when his cello parts for the album were recorded because his playing was so insanely beautiful. I wanted the cello to filter through the whole album and knew that if I ever got the chance to perform my own music live, I would have a cello in the lineup. That is the way it has been ever since. Martin and I wrote 'Montañas De Silencio' together, which eventually ended up on *What Lies Beneath*, and it was such a fast process, it was born in about half an hour.

Mel Wesson was another very important person on this album and we ended up working together on my next release as well. He's a sound designer and is behind all the eerie sounds and noises that make you jump during the scary parts of movies. He really helped me to capture the right atmosphere on 'My Little Phoenix', which was musically inspired by 'She Never Sleeps' from the soundtrack to *The Ring*, 'Lost Northern Star' and 'Damned and Divine'. Mel was surprised when I asked him to work with my music. He is usually involved in scores, mostly without vocals and often even without a song structure. But he embraced the challenge and did a superb job.

The first time I went to Zimmer's studios, I was really excited. *Gladiator* is one of my favourite soundtracks, so just being in that building, walking down those corridors and seeing all the movie posters on the walls was such an amazing experience. You might think recording studios are loud and chaotic, but everything was so calm and relaxed at Remote Control. Everybody worked quietly behind locked doors in their own individual studios; even if you walked along the corridor, you would barely hear any music. Listen carefully and you might sometimes hear a faint orchestra or strings or a bassoon as the team worked on movie soundtracks. I had one ear to the doors, sneaking around trying to figure out what they were working on. "This sounds like the next *Spiderman*!" While I was there they were soundtracking *Pirates of the Caribbean: At World's End* (2007). Coming from the classical world, I know about orchestras, but seeing how those guys work with the symphonic orchestras and what they add to the recordings is really spectacular. I gained so much knowledge from working in those studios.

ABOVE It was interesting to see all these awards hanging on the toilet walls at Remote Control Productions.

BELOW Martin Tillman is a magnificently emotional cello player and a huge part of my first solo record.

•◦————————◦•————————◦•

*a*s my first solo rock album, *My Winter Storm* was a huge project for me. It was recorded at 12 different locations, including Zimmer's Remote Control Productions studios, Rudolfinum in Prague (with the incredible Czech Film Orchestra) and Switzerland's Sound Development AG, Zurich. The album, and its follow-up, *What Lies Beneath*, were released through Universal Music and it was through them that I met so many of the musicians and songwriters I continue to work with today. When I departed Nightwish, I already had a relationship with the label. In 2005, Universal Music in Germany had released *Highest Hopes: The Best of Nightwish* and they had made a video of 'Sleeping Sun' to coincide with the release. The A&R guy who co-coordinated that shoot was Daniel Pieper, who ended up becoming my A&R at the beginning of my solo career.

Universal were looking forward to working with me on this new adventure, but what I had been doing in the band proved to be an early hurdle. I felt it would have been too obvious for me to just copy what I had already been doing in Nightwish, but that is what the label wanted me to do. Yet I thought differently. Why should I duplicate what had already been done? My vision was to do something new; to develop a new sound. I love heavy metal and I wanted to keep the guitars, but I also wanted the orchestra to sound as wonderful as possible, to have its own space

so that people could appreciate it. It is an incredibly difficult task to mix heavy metal guitars with an orchestra as both take up so much sound space, but I wanted my fans to get goosebumps as though they were listening to the soundtrack of a horror movie. It was a completely new idea and the only existing recordings I could find as examples were big movie soundtracks, which are structured very differently from metal songs. Yet I still wanted to keep those heavy metal elements because I love that style, too. The label needed to find someone who could meet me in the middle and that was producer Daniel Presley. He came from an alternative rock background and had worked with Faith No More, The Breeders and also Cradle of Filth – he is now a screenwriter and author. The two Daniels suggested some musicians, from which I picked bassist Doug Wimbish from Living Colour and guitarist Alex Scholpp from Farmer Boys. I had seen drummer Earl Harvin performing with Seal in Argentina and was very impressed, so he was my suggestion. Behind every instrument I needed a strong character with the knowledge and talent to help me realise my vision.

I was pretty nervous about starting from scratch again, but I felt free to make my own decisions and find my own way. When it came to creating my new music, the songwriting process was very different from what I had expected. It began with the label sending me demos for around 500 songs from which they wanted me to choose my favourites. I remember listening to the songs while I was driving: some were symphonic metal, some were weirder, and some were classical and the singer was pretending to be me. There were all sorts of songs and from those 500, I chose: 'I Walk Alone', 'My Little Phoenix', 'Sing for Me', 'Minor Heaven' and 'The Seer', which I ended up singing with Doro Pesch on the limited-edition 'The Seer' EP. We still needed more songs, though, and I wanted to write them. As I had not written any rock songs before, the label set up a songwriting camp in Ibiza. That turned into quite an experience.

ABOVE Some of the team behind the songs and production of my first album, including my A&R Daniel Pieper (second from right) and the producer Daniel Presley (third from right).

RIGHT I visited Anders and Matthias in Sweden to write more songs for my second album. Here we are at Anders' gorgeous summer cottage.

Doug Wimbish, bass

"It all started when I received an email from my accountant saying that an artist called Tarja was trying to contact me. She had seen my name on Annie Lennox's *Diva* and the Seal record [*Seal*] with Trevor Horn and she liked elements of those albums. I'd heard of Nightwish, but I wasn't familiar with the individuals in the band. Once I did some research, I completely fell in love with her voice. For me, Tarja's vocals crashing with metal, crashing with opera, crashing with theatre is perfection. Once we met, we just instantly got along. Funnily enough, I had already met her cello player, Max Lilja, a few years earlier when he was with Apocalyptica [he was their co-founder, now ex-member] and then, boom, we ended up in the same camp with Tarja.

"Things then happened really quickly. On *My Winter Storm*, we were trying to recreate what she could hear in her mind. She was experimenting; she knew what she wanted to do, but it was the first time she'd driven that car by herself and she needed other people to help interpret it for her, to help her find her balance. She was putting people together and seeing how it all connected. It was really interesting that on that first record, Alex Scholpp and I were able to lock together really quickly. The drummer Earl Harvin [Seal, Air] was coming from another frequency, but we recorded a series of songs and we enjoyed it. Out of that session came 'I Walk Alone' and to this day that is still one of her main songs.

"It was really fun making that first record because it was fresh and we had something new happening. When we arrived at the studio in Ireland, the client before us, just 48 hours before us, was Michael Jackson! We didn't see him but there were toys all over the place. [Jackson was recording his unreleased album with will.i.am in Westmeath, summer 2006. The

toys likely belonged to his children Prince Michael Junior, Paris and Prince Michael Jackson II, aka Blanket, who were there with nanny Grace and the children's tutor.]

"By the time we recorded the second album, *What Lies Beneath*, we had already toured. I was brought in as an ambiance director and that merged into how the band could function as a whole. There wasn't necessarily a need for this type of musical director, but at the time I was trying to share my experience with Tarja and perhaps offer something a little different from the usual. When we flew into Finland to record the album it was the middle of winter in snow, and Will Calhoun [Living Colour's drummer] joined me for some songs. Out of that record also came some great material. It's a bit more symphonic, and that allowed her classical opera skills to shine through. Tarja's sound could have been the soundtrack for a *Lord of the Rings* movie.

"Tarja has done a lot of great songs but 'Diva' was my favourite from the last tour – I like the theme of it and how the symphonic elements take place. It feels like I'm in a movie, like I'm on the sea or at a port, I feel like I'm a pirate in the Bahamas. I love the strings and the way it continues out from the bass. I love that song and it gives one a certain feeling.

"We've done some amazing shows and you could write the *Chronicles of Tarja* about all the different things she's done. One I remember was Luna Park in Argentina – that was great. First of all, there are great fans in Argentina. Tarja doesn't have to sing a note; they know all the lyrics and all the guitar parts as well – they're great fans! To me it was a highlight because it was her with an amazing production, packed hall and a stand-out performance. I remember playing another gig in

an armoury in La Paz [Bolivia, South America]. It's one of the highest cities on Earth and I got altitude sickness! During the show, I could hear all this cracking and popping and I'm, like, 'What's going on?' 'Oh, there's a civil war going on outside!' 'Outside where?' Outside the venue while we had the concert going on!

"Some of the most memorable shows were the ones we didn't get to play. We went to Chile in 2019 during a public protest and the gig got cancelled. We arrived the night before and saw the club we were supposed to be playing in, but the buildings on either side were burned out. That was very challenging. We did Venezuela and for one of the gigs in Caracas we found out that the future president of El Salvador was supposed to visit the hotel we were staying in. We were on the 20th floor and all of a sudden I see this rope dangle outside my window, and then these blackout guys with machine guns coming down the rope and I'm like, 'What is going on?' I look outside and the highway is shut. I go downstairs and it's full-on. You've got the paramilitary police over here and some folks were saying, 'You can't use that elevator.' Turns out that Hugo Chávez had flown in to our hotel in a helicopter to meet the president-elect from El Salvador.

"I have so many great memories from cutting those albums and the tours. That was a good chunk of time, enough time to be able to put out a product and deal with the press, deal with the reality of how this industry is. Because it's a cruel industry and I was starting to see what was happening to Tarja in the press. Uncle Dougie didn't like it one bit. There are three sides to every story: what you say, what I say and what really happened. There were times when I would just give Tarja a hug and ask her what's happening. She'd say, 'Dougie, I'm not OK.' And I'd tell her not to worry about it and to just hang in there.

"As a friend, you always find ways to be patient and you find the correct moments to spend with them to help defuse the ticking time bombs of tension. You have to find peace in your life. Tarja's still here and she's been able to survive it all. She endured Finland and all the challenges that were there post-Nightwish. I'm thankful for that. She was able to survive the opinions of others. Being in a band is like being part of a family, but bands can also be like dysfunctional families. If you don't deal with something at that time, it festers. I guess I try to bring my life experience as an elder; I'm a bass player, an ambience director and Uncle Dougie!"

I was there for less than two weeks with three different teams of writers. Among them were Anders Wollbeck and Mattias Lindblom, who had already written 'I Walk Alone' and 'Minor Heaven' with Hanne Sørvaag. I fell in love with 'I Walk Alone', which became the first single, as soon as I heard it. The album title comes from this line in the song: "My winter storm/Holding me awake, it's never gone." There is a lot of positivity in that song and those lines connected with my childhood in Finland: I have lived through so many winter storms. For me, my fans are my winter storm, holding me awake, and I never walk alone while my fans are there for me.

ABOVE With Torsten, while we were working on the songs for my first album. We wrote 'Damned and Divine' and 'The Reign' together.

Although the final lyrics were close to the original version, Matthias was very kind to let me introduce a few twists to make the song relate to me personally. Nowadays I always laugh with Matthias about his original vision for the song when he wrote the lyrics, and where it ended up when I was done with it. It has become a very important song for me.

Also part of the songwriting camp in Ibiza were duo Kiko Masbaum and Michelle Leonard, while the dance producer Torsten Stenzel and his then wife Angela Heldmann and Adrian Zagoritis made up the third team. I was literally running from one studio to another and panicking because time was running out. One guy would make me a demo of the background music and I would sing the melody. We would say, "Yes, this is a good idea, let's go with that!" And then I would run to another camp to work on a different song. It was crazy. I was writing with new people who did not know who I was, what my tastes were, or what was between my ears.

One of my aims was to try to go beneath the surface and write interesting, deep lyrics. When it comes to this process, I find the author Paulo Coelho very inspirational. I've read his books so many times, but the first one I read was *The Alchemist*, which I sent to my brothers to read as well. I love the way he talks about life and I can connect to his philosophy in so many ways. Paulo's work has a recurrent theme relating to dreams and how your life is pushed forward when you pursue them. He writes about dreams in the form of short stories, a long novel or even just a couple of lines. I didn't discover the world of dreams through reading Paulo's books, but it was gratifying to read about them in a way that's similar to how I live my life. Paulo's work inspired me to write about dreams in my lyrics as an ongoing theme, one that I could approach in many different ways, either disguised by real events or in fantasy stories.

LEFT Straight after Matias from Mandinga Tattoo finished his amazing work on my 'Die Alive tattoo. I couldn't be happier with the outcome.

BELOW Talking about Paulo Coelho's influence on my work on the day his book, *Aleph*, was launched in Finland. The first song from *Outlanders* (see page 196), on which we used Paulo's words, was played for the audience at the book launch.

'The Reign' is an excellent example of where I combined the ideas that were sparked by reading *The Alchemist* with my own longing for the sea and my wishes and troubles at the time. The song title 'Die Alive' comes from an interview I read with Paulo where he told the journalist that you should live your life fully every moment of the day, so that when your time comes, you die alive. I could relate to that – I even have 'Die Alive' tattooed on my arm. Paulo and I have since become acquaintances and he's been really supportive of my work.

To my frustration, however, some of the writers were coming up with really cheesy ideas. For them, heavy metal had bombastic, galloping double-kick drums, fanfares, high-pitched screams and so on. In modern metal, you would never see anyone using these in such a clichéd way. It was very stressful, but I managed to get the songs to a place I was comfortable with. I was completely exhausted after those couple of weeks and decided I would never write songs in such a chaotic way again.

I always try to find the positive in everything, though, and this album and the production process taught me such a lot that I knew would serve me well in my solo career. I was very happy with the album at the time – it is a real piece of art – but of course if I had had the knowledge and experience I

RIGHT With Uwe Flade, director of the video for 'Die Alive'.

BELOW We filmed the video for 'Die Alive' in an abandoned Soviet Union military base in Berlin, Germany. It was freezing and we had a campfire to keep us warm through the night.

ABOVE My shell beach in Antigua.
I have written countless melodies here.

do now, there are things I would have done differently. Despite the bad experiences I had in Ibiza, I did establish several lasting friendships there. I still work with Anders and have since written more lyrics with Mattias. I also became great friends with Torsten and Angela. After Ibiza, they moved to Antigua in the Caribbean, and my husband Marcelo and I ended up buying a summer house there, too.

Through these new songs, I was able to weave my own stories by creating four different characters: The Dead Boy, The Doll, The Phoenix and The Ice Queen. Although I did not admit it at the time, they all represented different parts of me during that period. I was not yet willing to reveal too much about myself, so I focused on becoming the storyteller for these characters, who all appear on the album's artwork. The Ice Queen is a very strong character who is powerful but very helpful and kind; The Dead Boy is very sad and troubled; The Phoenix is, of course, myself reborn; and then there is The Doll, an ironic image, who is a sort of marionette with someone else holding the strings – as I have myself at times been incorrectly portrayed. These characters gave me a way to connect to the songs and bring deeper personal meaning to the lyrics.

Of course, not all of the songs on *My Winter Storm* are original; among them is a cover of Alice Cooper's 'Poison', which was my idea. Back when I was going through the demos the record company sent me, the rock radio station in Finland was playing 'Poison' on rotation and it became a running joke for me to hear that song three or four times a day. During every break I had from listening and researching my own material, 'Poison' was there. I took it as a sign. I have always enjoyed singing cover versions and thought, "Do I dare to cover this?" I enlisted some of my friends to sing backing vocals, including my younger brother, so it was a fun project to do.

A few years later, on my 2010 *What Lies Beneath* tour, I supported Alice Cooper in Europe and of course I told him that I had covered or, more accurately, transformed his song into something else! He was such a gentleman and was very kind to me and my team. I remember one day there was a lot of press following him and when he saw me in the corridor, he yelled, "And that's the best voice in this industry!"

ABOVE The only tour I have done in my solo career as a support act was with Alice Cooper for his 2010 concerts in Germany. It was a huge pleasure to meet Alice in person.

◆◆———◆◆————◆◆

*t*he writing process in Ibiza had been stressful but things were about to get even more challenging. I soon realised that neither my producer, Daniel Presley, nor the label really understood my cinematic vision for the album. They saw me as just another heavy metal warrior, but I did not want to be put in a box and I faced a huge struggle to be heard.

The orchestrated songs that I had worked on at Remote Control Productions sounded amazing – 'I Walk Alone', 'The Reign', and so on. Mixing engineer Slamm Andrews had given them all a killer sound, like they belonged on a movie soundtrack. (Slamm would go on to mix part of my second rock album, *What Lies Beneath,* as well.) But for the rest of the album it was agreed that I, with my classical training, would handle the orchestra, choir and sound designs elements. Daniel would concentrate on producing and recording the band to ensure we did not lose the heavy metal side of things. However, Daniel also really helped me structure 'Oasis' (the only track I wrote entirely on my own) before we sent it to Jim Dooley for the orchestration.

In keeping with my concept, I wanted several of the songs to have their own intros and outros as a way of setting the mood and allowing them to breathe, but the label wanted to chop them shorter to create snappier radio edits. Marcelo and I went through the album separating these short instrumental sections into individual tracks – that's why we ended up with 'Ite, Missa Est'

(which comes before 'I Walk Alone'), 'Seeking for the Reign', 'The Escape of the Doll' and 'Sunset' on the track listing. I really fought hard for my vision but everything I did had to go through my producer. To make sure his role was not undermined, I was not allowed to speak directly to my band and tell them what I wanted, which was very frustrating.

The band parts were recorded at Grouse Lodge Studios in Ireland and despite the communication issues, it was so relaxed there with lots of lush green fields surrounding it. It is a very important studio: Michael Jackson has worked there as well as Tom Jones, Muse and REM. Torsten, my musicians, Doug, Alex and Earl, and I gathered in the studio to work on the album and it was really nice to be together – it gave me the sense of having a proper band lineup. I even wrote 'Ciarán's Well' there at the last minute with Alex. There was a well near the studio that he discovered by accident while taking a walk after one of our heavy recording sessions. It was Ciarán's Well, of course, and I thought it would be interesting to create a story around it, with ancient forests and a mythical fairy. He came up with a great riff, and I said, "Hey, let's write a song!" I needed a metal kick and it was very spontaneous.

I went back to Ibiza to record the vocals. It was super-hot, which is great because my voice always sounds better if there is humidity in the air. Because of what happened with my first Christmas

ABOVE The gang who worked on my first album with me at Grouse Lodge Studios, Ireland. I was so happy to record my first album with these talented people.

OPPOSITE I loved the peaceful, rural surroundings of Grouse Lodge. It is hard to think of a nicer place to be creative.

BELOW St. Ciaran's Well – our inspiration for the song of the same name.

LEFT I am pretty critical when it comes to my own vocal recordings.

BELOW It was amazing to bring these guys – all from different backgrounds – together to record *My Winter Storm*. I am grateful to have them in my life.

album, I told the label that I was not comfortable recording vocals in a studio, so we did them in a rented house. This came with its own problems. We recorded live takes with the monitor behind the microphone, so it felt like I had an orchestra with me in the room. But that setup meant that you could hear all the ambient noises, such as the cicadas chirping in the trees. We did not check how many decibels they were exactly, but at times they were ridiculously loud. I remember Marcelo running out of the house with a hosepipe and spraying water into the trees while I was recording indoors.

Aside from the background noise, I did not like the fact that the producer was editing my vocals. My voice has a natural vibrato, but he was editing it out, which meant my vocals were clipped. You cannot imagine how painful that was for me. I needed to trust his abilities, to trust that he was going to do a good job – I had to. But my voice does not sound as I would have loved it to sound on that album, and since then I have never edited my vocals like that again. We should have spent a month recording the album but we didn't even finish it because he was editing my vocals all the time. I ended up recording new vocals in the Village Studios in LA while I was working at Remote Control Productions with the orchestra arrangers. That was another lesson learned: never work with a person who cannot understand you as a singer.

Despite the ups and downs, there was plenty to celebrate as I finished my first solo album. After being fired from the band I had helped to create, I'd lost all trust in humanity; I was a wreck and needed to start making music with people I didn't know. It took me a long time to regain my trust in people. I had all the doubts in the world: "What if that person is stabbing me in the back after two months' work?" I did not trust anybody, so I have been very lucky to find amazing professionals, talented people who I call my family when we're on the road. Although, of course, there have been occasions where people have not got along or something has gone wrong.

From having nothing, I ended up having everything: a live band I am very close to, and an album of my own songs to perform for the first time – it was the whole package, everything was ready for the future. It was a huge amount of work, but it was done in a short period of time.

My Winter Storm was released on November 19, 2007, and less than a week later we began the *Storm* world tour in Berlin. We toured Europe three times, South America twice and North America, too. I was on the

OPPOSITE The rented house in Ibiza where we recorded *My Winter Storm* – not a very glamorous setting for the vocal recordings, but this was how we wanted to do it back then.

LEFT The trip to Eilat, Israel, will live long in our memories. I rented a yacht for a day and invited my band and crew to join me for scuba diving, snorkelling, jet skiing and fun.

BELOW The very beginning of a show during the *What Lies Beneath* world tour. I loved appearing in a mask.

road constantly but it was such an insanely beautiful experience that I would often burst into tears of happiness during it!

On the first leg of that tour, my younger brother Toni played drums, guitars, keyboards and sang 'Phantom of the Opera' with me. The Finnish keyboard player Maria Ilmoniemi also performed with me, which I loved as I was not used to sharing the stage with a woman during my rock tours.

The tour was a very emotional experience but it gave me confidence because I realised that so many promoters were interested in working with me. It was an excellent start and it proved to me that I could do this. I had a makeup artist with me too, which was such a luxury and one I'd never had before. I also performed an acoustic set for the first time, with just

BELOW All over the world, but especially in Russia, the Ukraine, Belarus and Eastern European countries, people always send me flowers. Sometimes their beauty takes my breath away.

my voice and the piano. I remember the first time I sat behind the keyboard to play a stripped-down version of 'Oasis' to my rock audience, and they were so supportive. My fans gave me such love and I needed that, I needed to grow and gain confidence.

The *Storm* tour lasted two years and during that time, I released a special UK-only 'The Seer' EP with extra live tracks as well as a fan edition of *My Winter Storm* which contained a new song called 'Enough', written with Kiko and Michelle. I recorded it on tour in Buenos Aires with my live band, which was an amazing experience. The extended edition of 'Enough' contained another song called 'Wisdom of Wind', co-written by film composer Jeff Rona and Dead Can Dance's Lisa Gerrard, who co-wrote the *Gladiator* soundtrack with Hans Zimmer. It was a beautiful song and I was so happy that he gave me permission to use it on this special release.

When we came to the end of the touring cycle, I was exhausted but invigorated at the same time. I had been writing songs for the next album between tour dates and was ready to be productive again. I had a plan: I wanted the musicians to feel more connected to the project and I wanted to record it with everyone in the same studio, like a proper band. Which is exactly what I did.

ABOVE It was great having all the band together to record in the studio in Buenos Aires. We were on tour in South America at the time, so we took the chance to record the song 'Enough'. Here you can see the beginning of the love story of Kiko (seated with guitar) and Maria (keyboards). Recording engineer Mario Altamirano, who has always helped me out with my sessions in Argentina, is getting ready to record Doug's parts of the song.

BELOW I felt amazing when I was given this German Gold Award during my show in Summerbreeze, Germany. I couldn't believe I was the first Finnish solo artist to win this award. You all made this happen and I am truly grateful.

4

what
LIES
beneath

ABOVE My escape: diving. When I
was under the water, I totally forgot
all my worries and stresses.

I have always loved being near the water, I find it relaxing and it soothes my soul. As a child, I was surrounded by water and would spend the summer months swimming in the lakes in Finland. I am not an amazing swimmer but in 2006, I began scuba diving and loved it. It was one of the few times that I did not think about my work, I was just there listening to my own breath, relaxing and enjoying the moment. It took me away from everything – that is the beauty of it. The best places to dive are where the water is crystal clear and warm – in Egypt, the Caribbean, the Maldives and the Indian Ocean – although I have also done it in the freezing waters of Argentina or Finland, in muddy water where you cannot see anything.

Sadly, a few years ago I was diagnosed with an ear problem and my doctor advised me to stop scuba diving because it could damage my hearing. I have therefore given it up, although I still snorkel whenever I can. My husband is an advanced diver and my daughter is a great swimmer too, she loves snorkelling with us. Under the water, colours are so different: the blues and corals so much brighter, and underneath the coral are so many amazing sea creatures which you might otherwise miss. There is so much life there and it was the underwater world that inspired my second rock album, *What Lies Beneath.*

The theme of this album was that, one way or another, we are all living on the surface; we do not dare to explore what lies beneath. We do not look in the mirror and really accept who we are. I wanted to explore the notion of what we discover when we look a little deeper. I wrote songs dealing with darker topics, such as child abuse and how you can live with someone who has that kind of darkness within them and you do not know it, until suddenly it comes into the light. For 'In for a Kill', I wrote about the hidden practice of shark-killing in Asia – again, that came from me being a scuba diver and nature lover. (Incidentally, it is an in-house joke with Matthias, Anders and myself that this song is our version of a James Bond theme in the style of the classics 'Thunderball', 'Diamonds are Forever' or 'A View to a Kill'.) These themes came from watching the news and from talking to people and hearing their stories. Some of it came from within, too, from asking, "Am I ready to reveal myself?" What was it that lay inside me, in my heart and my soul? At that time, I was looking in the mirror and wondering if I was ready or capable of being a solo artist, and I had all the doubts in the world.

The album took about two years to create while I worked between tour dates. I had enjoyed touring with my first rock album, and although I was feeling more grounded and more confident, I was still learning and that is why this album ended up being more experimental.

I mainly wrote the album in three different locations: Finland, where we had just built a home with a dedicated studio; Buenos Aires, where we had moved into a newly built apartment; and Antigua. I was far more relaxed on this album. Although I was not yet ready to write a whole album on my own, that would come as I grew in confidence. Naturally, I wanted to collaborate once more with the songwriters and musicians I had enjoyed working with on *My Winter Storm*.

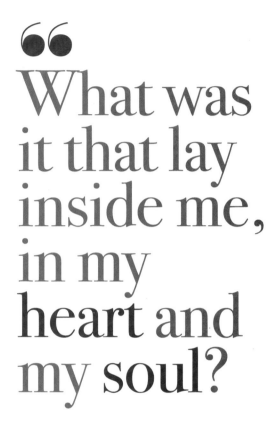

"

What was it that lay inside me, in my heart and my soul?

LEFT My wall of work and it's all because of my fans. I thank you!

ABOVE Writing songs for *What Lies Beneath* with Kiko Masbaum and Michelle Leonard in Antigua.

BELOW With songwriters for *What Lies Beneath*, Angela Heldmann and Adrian Zagoritis, in Antigua.

The first songs that I wrote for the new album were created on the Caribbean island of Antigua, with Torsten and Angela. The ocean is very inspiring and it was a beautiful experience to sit on the beach, singing melodies into my iPhone. When I listen back to the demos I can hear the waves in the background.

If you think of darker or heavy metal music, you might not connect that to a beach location or palm trees, but there is something about Antigua that I find so stimulating. There is a really positive energy there. My family can sense it, too: I feel good there and never suffer headaches, for instance – perhaps because it's so far away from the chaos of everything, and the pollution.

One of the earliest songs I wrote for *What Lies Beneath* was 'Naiad', about a water nymph, and that is where the title of the album comes from, although that track doesn't appear on the original version of the album. I was taking a break at a local coffee shop and picked up a magazine that someone had left on the table. On the cover was a beautiful water sculpture by a British artist called Jason deCaires Taylor. Over time, coral grows on these sculptures and they start to re-shape: they look creepy but inspired me to write a fantasy story for this song. Inside, the article had the headline "What Lies Beneath" – it was perfect and connected all the songs I had already written.

'The Archive of Lost Dreams' was another song connected to the underwater fantasy world and the character of the water nymph that I had created for 'Naiad'. With its piano accompaniment, the track was conceived almost like a score for a movie, with the images playing in my head, rather than on a screen. I find the grand piano a very inspiring instrument and there has been one at my home ever since I worked on this album. I have a Bechstein and it's a very smooth-sounding instrument, it has a film-score quality to it and is very easy to play. Every time I do, it frees my mind and I have to make sure there's a recording device next to me because there is nearly always something that comes out. It is a fantastic feeling to be able to free yourself with just one instrument.

Marta Blanco, singing teacher

"I was introduced to Tarja in the early 2010s by some colleagues who recommended me as a singing teacher. I usually work in the world of classical and lyrical music and didn't know anything about her before we met, but I immediately fell in love with her voice because it's so warm and beautiful. She's an excellent student and practises hard until she's able to solve any issues she may have. She's very focused and her voice has really developed over the years, becoming much more flexible and versatile.

"Tarja has a real passion for performing classical music with orchestras and choirs – even during her rock performances. By no means is it an easy thing to do, and really demonstrates her technical preparation and hard work. When she first told me she wanted to record an album of *Ave Maria* prayers, I thought it would be an excellent way to present her classical repertoire to her existing fans, as well as new ones. I helped her to prepare for the album and was present during the recording. We had such a wonderful time and the results are truly worth celebrating.

"The way to prepare the voice for singing is always the same, regardless of the style of music. Breathing well is the top priority, and you need to use your voice in the correct way, without straining or forcing it. The best advice I can give to young classical singers is to study your voice with love and patience. You're only given one voice in your life, and singing will provide you with an extraordinary way of enjoying it."

ABOVE Working with my singing teacher Marta Blanco, who flew from Buenos Aires to help me during the recordings of *Ave Maria - en Plein Air*. Her unconditional support and knowledge has been really important to me in my career.

Of course, as a singer, my voice is my most important instrument. At that time, I was having singing lessons maybe once or twice a month. I had a coach in Buenos Aires, called Marta Blanco, who I would see when I was there, and when I moved to Buenos Aires permanently I would see her every two weeks. I still have singing lessons with her but nowadays I call her when I am working on a classical production that requires really accurate work. Thanks to the constant training, my voice was changing all the time, and becoming more flexible. At the beginning of my career, with Nightwish, my voice was lower and darker and I was still a mezzo soprano because that was the only sound I could make at that time. Now, my voice was getting stronger where it needed to be and lighter where that was required, too: I found I could handle those changes in dynamic a little better. I was also becoming more confident in my performances and was generally much happier with everything in my life.

As well as Antigua, I travelled to Berlin to write with Michelle and Kiko, and to Sweden to work with Mattias and Anders – I went to Anders' summer cottage and to their studio in Stockholm as well. I also wrote 'Little Lies' with my guitarist Alex, but at that stage I was not writing with anyone else in the band. Johnny Andrews was a new face; he was introduced to me because of his relationship with Finnish rock band The 69 Eyes and Finnish classical-meets-metal band Apocalyptica and I had a very good feeling about him. We met for the first time in LA and talked about music, then I invited him to Finland and together we wrote some very important songs for the album, including 'Until My Last Breath', 'Underneath', 'Falling Awake' and 'Dark Star'.

Even though I cannot write a complete song while I'm on tour, I am still thinking about music and gathering ideas. When I was touring *My Winter Storm* in Turkey, it was a very powerful experience to walk along the streets in Istanbul and hear the Muslim community praying several times a day. I wanted to record this so I could use it on a record one day. It ended up in 'Dark Star' – thankfully, my iPhone recording was in the right key! It was just perfect.

For me, songwriting is a mixture of solo and collaborative work. The way I usually work is by first mapping out the songs on my piano or keyboard, recording some ideas at home and then making a demo. I can only compose when I am alone. I need that space around me and even though I have written songs when my daughter has been running around in the background, I have headphones on and a keyboard in front of me turned up loud. She lets me work, she doesn't really disturb me. But in general, I need to have my own space and my own time so that the creative juices can flow. It is not like pressing a button and the music comes out. Working under pressure is never a good way to write. I experienced that on the first album and it was not something I wanted to repeat.

When I have made the demo, I share it with my musicians and tell them what I want to do. This is very much the way I work now and I've found that a lot of other musicians work in this way, too. To make music for a poem or text that already exists would be different, and I don't know if it would be more difficult or not because in my case, the music speaks to me first and I create the stories and lyrics second.

For that part I enjoy working with songwriters because then it is not only your soul involved. I cannot read another person's mind and many unexpected and magical elements come up. It is really beautiful when you connect with someone in that way. For example, when I was writing lyrics with Mattias, at first we would brainstorm and talk, and then start writing.

Having rented a house for recording vocals for *My Winter Storm*, I wanted to have my own vocal room, so we built one in Finland. I also recorded some vocals in Buenos Aires but we recorded the rest of the album at Petrax

Studios in Hollola, Finland, where Apocalyptica and Children of Bodom have also recorded. Owned by a Finnish couple, Tiina and Petri Rappula, the studio is on a farm in the middle of nowhere and we lived and slept above the studio so we could work until very late.

With Doug and Alex alongside me in the studio, it felt like the old days. I also invited Will Calhoun from Living Colour to the studio. This was the first album that I made with Max Lilja (ex-Apocalyptica), Mike Terrana and Christian Kretschmar, who were all part of my live lineup at the time. I had originally met Christian through German electronic band Schiller and asked if he would join me for a few shows. Luckily for me, he said yes. He's super-talented, playing keyboards, Hammond organ, piano and cello as well – and has been with me ever since.

I knew these guys a little already, but I wanted to get to know them even better. It was also a matter of trust; I wanted to trust them and for them to trust me. Living together there was a real bonding experience and we developed a fantastic relationship. There were always last-minute changes taking place: some days we were dead tired and just went straight to bed with no time for partying. It was very cold and there was a lot of snow, so we would often go for walks and play with the studio dog. For the Americans, Doug and Will, it was their first time recording in Finland and I don't think they had ever been surrounded by so much snow before.

ABOVE This was the scenery surrounding us while we were recording the *What Lies Beneath* album in Hollola, Finland. Stepping out of the Petrax Studios, only silence and wind was there to greet you.

BELOW When we started recording the vocals for my second album, I decided to try out several microphones. Although many famous singers consider some of these to be the best, the most expensive ones were just not working for my voice. It is dynamic and not all of the mics were able to handle its subtle changes. For a long time, my partner in crime has been the Røde K-2.

Occasionally, I miss those times and really wish we could do that again. It was such a beautiful time with so many inspiring people and so much brainstorming taking place. We recorded two drummers at the same time for the song 'Crimson Deep', just like they used to do in the 70s, because I wanted to have a massive organic sound with two great drummers, and Will and Mike were talking about how to do it – moments like these are so special.

('Crimson Deep' was also one of the songs that reconnected me with Remote Control Productions. The music was written with Bart Hendrickson, who had worked on *The Ring Two* soundtrack – as a fellow metalhead he was super-easy to write with.)

ABOVE One day, in Petrax Studios, my friend from Harus' lineup, Marzi Nyman, came to delight us with his pedals and guitar work.

OPPOSITE My brother Timo almost swallowed a fly while we were working on the backing vocals for the 'Still of the Night' cover for *What Lies Beneath*.

*a*lthough it is wonderful to have a regular team, one-off collaborations allow you to create something really unique. For instance, for 'Anteroom of Death' I was looking for a really freaky vocal arrangement in the middle-eight of the song and I love working on vocal arrangements with choirs. The song was begging for me to go way bigger, but where to go? I had an idea to use Venetian carnival masks on the album artwork to symbolise what lies beneath, like in a theatre play. The song was already crazy enough with tempo changes and a reggae part, but I still wanted to give it a Queen's 'Bohemian Rhapsody' vocal treatment. I had heard the German a cappella group Van Canto performing a cover version of Nightwish's 'Wishmaster' and thought they could be amazing. Which they were. It was great to work with them.

I would never try to write a song like 'Anteroom of Death' again – in fact, I would never try to repeat any of my songs. Many bands do that and are very successful because of it, but I hate repeating myself;

I always want to create something new. It is an incredible challenge and really satisfying when you see the results. Pushing the boundaries like this is more artistic and more valuable to me. I have always been a fighter and I have always worked very hard. Through my lyrics, I have always encouraged people to believe in themselves and to fight for that.

For 'Falling Awake', I worked with American rock musician Joe Satriani and he was really kind. When I approached him with the idea of working together, I wanted to meet up with him but he was too busy and said, "Give me a couple of days" with the track, and he came back with this solo. In order to work with him, I asked my friend Julian Barrett from Buenos Aires – who has played guitar for me ever since this album – to record a guide solo as a reference for Joe, but I loved it so much we ended up using it in another version of the song, too. Of course, while my brothers were super-impressed by what their sister was doing, they were even more proud when they learned I was working with Joe Satriani! When we had the two versions ready, my record company in the UK asked me if I would like to have Jason Hook from Five Finger Death Punch play the solo for a special UK release. I am a fan of the band and love Jason's sound, so I agreed straight away. And that is how we ended up having three different guitar players and solos for the same song! This is a great example of one of the positive sides of being a solo artist: you can do as you see fit instead of being restricted by the often more rigid structure of a band.

My brothers were involved on this album, and both sang backing vocals on my cover of Whitesnake's 'Still of the Night'. I love Whitesnake so much, I was a fan and listened to them in my youth because my older brother listened to them. This was one of the songs that was always playing on my portable cassette player. I had always felt that if I covered it, I would make it more symphonic, so I wrote a new part for the song, a huge orchestral section in the middle-eight that is not in the

Although it is **wonderful** to have a regular team, one-off collaborations allow you to create something **really unique**.

original. It was the way I heard it in my head, and it was a challenge vocally because it was written for a male singer, but I really wanted to tackle it.

Rock gods aside, the album also took inspiration from the King of Pop, Michael Jackson, who had recently passed away. The whole world seemed to collapse after the news was announced, but the truth is that only a few months earlier the media were not treating Michael that kindly, nor were his achievements being celebrated. I wanted to write a song about how sometimes we are not considered until something happens. I am talking about his career, his music, his videos – somehow he needed to die before some people were reminded of his work. It seemed that in dying he added value to his career when not long before nobody had cared as much. The result was 'Until My Last Breath', which I wrote with Johnny Andrews in Finland.

Although the first single of the album was 'Falling Awake', which acted as a warm-up and a little reveal of the new sound *What Lies Beneath* was about to present, I wanted Universal in Germany to release 'Until My Last Breath' as the second, and main, single. That was the strategy we had agreed upon, but they brought in a last-minute song called 'I Feel Immortal'. The lyrics were not anything I would sing about and it just was not me, so I told them, "If you want me to do this song, you have to give me the freedom to work on it." I was already deep in the stages of production, but Johnny and I fixed the lyrics and changed it to suit my voice, making it more operatic. It is a nice song and I do like it, but I still believe 'Until My Last Breath' was the better choice. Even within the same record company, some territories decided to go with it instead of 'I Feel Immortal'. In the end, this simultaneous release of different singles didn't work out as expected. It was not the first disagreement I had with Universal Music and, as much as

IT SEEMED THAT IN DYING HE ADDED VALUE TO HIS CAREER

I acknowledge their good intentions and genuine interest, our visions did not always concur. I even had a bet about how the single they chose was going to perform and won a dinner with one of the high-ranked bosses of the company...

✦━━━━━*✦*━━━━━*✦*

*m*y aim for *What Lies Beneath* was to make it pretty heavy, taking inspiration from American metal bands including Disturbed, Avenged Sevenfold or Five Finger Death Punch. I was also listening to a lot of In Flames at the time (and still do). This time I was involved in the songwriting and production of all the songs, and I had a particular sound in mind for each one. For instance, 'Naiad' is very different from 'In For a Kill' and that is very different again from 'Dark Star' or 'Crying Moon' – those are such powerful songs. It was therefore very important to me to work with three different mixing engineers on the album. The first album had been a huge challenge for Slamm because, as well as cinematographic, symphonic songs, there were rock songs that required a heavy metal band production sound, and Slamm was not particularly experienced in mixing these types of songs. I could not make certain tracks sound as heavy as I wanted, so this time I wanted to do things differently.

I agreed that Slamm would mix the orchestral songs because he could achieve that symphonic, film-score sound. I also adored the sound that Colin Richardson had created on the Slipknot albums, and I knew which songs I wanted him to work on. Then I enlisted a new engineer, Tim Palmer, who I had not worked with but whose sound I knew from his work with the Finnish band HIM, to work on 'Until My Last Breath'. He had a poppier sound, so I thought it would be perfect in his hands. With all three mixing engineers, I sat next to them in the studio – working with Colin, I learned that it was the first time he had mixed a track with a symphonic orchestra.

I was not afraid of mixing the album with three engineers, but even that got the record company nervous. They were having doubts about how that was going to work on the same album. But it was crystal clear for me: each engineer was going to mix the songs that were in the style they were best at. I was very direct with them, and they were all very open-minded. Tim invited me and my family into his home in Austin, Texas. I was there in his home studio with Marcelo for weeks and it was really lovely. Some of the mixing was done in the

UK with Colin at London's Miloco Studios, and the rest was done in LA with Slamm at Remote Control. Mel Wesson also played a big role in adding the soundtrack quality to this album with his sound design and programming, just as he had done with *My Winter Storm*.

From the very start, I knew I wanted to produce this album on my own. After *My Winter Storm*, I realised that there is no one who knows what I want and how I want to do things better than myself. Once recording started, I was very nervous about whether I could pull this off, but my husband and the musicians who already knew me were there beside me. I loved every moment. I wanted to try out techniques I had heard other producers and other musicians use, so I was very experimental in the production and did things that I felt were right at the time for that album. I drew on all the knowledge from my studies, and it was really fulfilling to discover that I was capable of achieving that level of production – it was a real highlight for me.

Since then, I have produced all my own albums. Production is such an important stage of the recording process. Once the songs have been written, I send them to everybody and then take control, whether online or in the studio. My musicians have no idea what I am going to do with the recordings once they send them back to me, so it is always a surprise to them when they get to hear the finished tracks.

The release of *What Lies Beneath* on August 31, 2010, marked the end of my relationship with Universal Music and the beginning of a new musical chapter in my life. I had realised that the end of our collaboration was near. I wanted more freedom to create my brand of heavy rock music but also I wanted to expand my boundaries outside of rock. Universal Music were still interested in renewing our agreement, but I needed a partner who could understand me and share my vision.

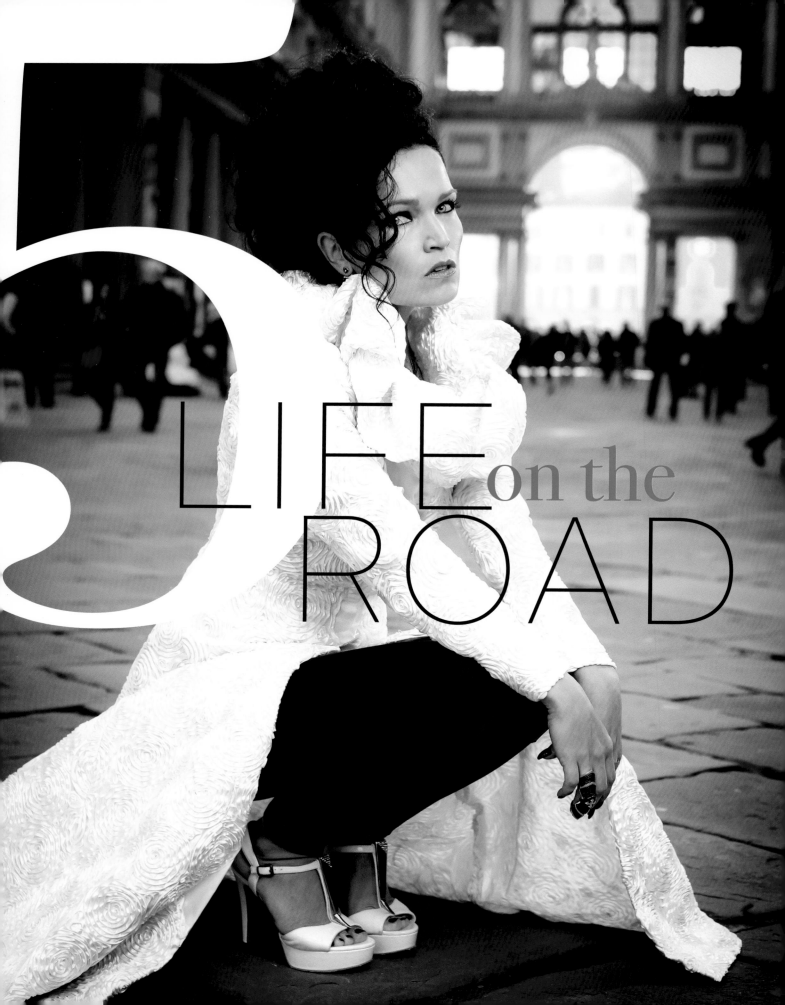

5

LIFE on the
ROAD

When I first began performing live, I never imagined that I would have to worry about getting shot onstage or kidnapped – but I have played in some very dangerous places where either could have happened.

In 2017, I toured Central America for the first time, which was very exciting, if slightly scary at times. We visited Honduras, El Salvador and Guatemala and found that even when in a hotel in those countries we'd often hear the sound of gunshots outside. El Salvador is very dangerous and has lots of drug gangs. When we were there the hotel staff told us to never leave the building alone and I had to make sure all my crew took that seriously, because their lives are my responsibility. One of the guys did not believe me, though, and went to buy some cigarettes from a kiosk 200 metres from the hotel. I knew that as soon as he stepped foot outside, people would be watching him. I was so thankful that nothing bad happened on that occasion, but I was very angry with him.

However, that fear was nothing compared to the very first time we landed at Toncontin Airport in Honduras. I will never forget it. I have never much liked flying but as we started to make our descent, I was shocked when I noticed that the passengers near me looked really scared and were crossing themselves. It was only afterwards that the captain announced that this was one of the most dangerous areas to land because it has a very short runway and is really close to the mountains. Once we got off the plane, there were more surprises as everywhere we looked there were guards holding machine guns. The country has one of the highest homicide rates in the world and you need security there 24/7. It is a completely different experience from touring Europe.

I got used to the extra security fairly quickly, though. When I went to Russia for the first time, there was a security guard following me everywhere to make sure

ABOVE This is how crazy it gets sometimes outside the venues – I love my fans.

I was safe; he even waited for me behind the toilet door and outside my hotel room. It makes me feel very secure but it is not a nice feeling to be followed by these huge military guys. (If I told my father these stories, he would never let me go anywhere again!) When people ask me why I go to these places, I reply that it's because I want to make my fans feel good, no matter where they live and what sort of hell they are going through. I am not afraid, and have walked through the audience while singing, with people touching me as I pass. Music is liberating, it is beautiful and connects us all and I can't let fear hold me back.

When I made my first live performance at the age of six I never dreamed that I would eventually have the chance to sing on so many different stages all over the world. My solo career has seen me perform in countries I had never been before, often performing in front of thousands of people and supporting many legendary bands. I have had some truly amazing experiences and hope there will be many more. In 2011, I played at Sonisphere Festival in France and it was only afterwards that I realised I had just shared the bill with Megadeth and Metallica. My teenage self would have never believed it. I remember warming up in the trailer next to the Megadeth guys and hearing one of them say, "Ah, that's the operatic chick." Wow, it was such an amazing feeling.

One of the most memorable concerts I have played (so far) was in Indonesia. I was the only female singer at Hammersonic Festival and it was amazing to see all the women in the front row rocking out. They were wearing niqabs, with only their eyes exposed, and I felt like a superwoman helping them to feel empowered. That was so different from anywhere else I have performed. I have toured Asia and have played some very special places, including Japan, Hong Kong, Thailand and China. My fans there are so much quieter than my followers in South America, but they are just as passionate.

Back when *My Winter Storm* came out, I played my very first show at the Festivalna Hall in Sofia, Bulgaria, and I remember crying before I went onstage because there were 4,000 people in the audience, and I could not believe they had all come to see me. Ever since that moment, the country has welcomed me with open arms, and I have performed all my albums for them. I played at Kavarna Rock in 2010, which is a festival in the northeastern part of the country, and later found out that my face is painted on the side of one of the apartment blocks there. It is such an honour to be part of famous metal murals that feature Ronnie James Dio, Alice Cooper, Lemmy and Dave Mustaine. I was so proud when I found out, especially because, as far as I know, I am the only woman among those male legends.

ABOVE The show in Santiago de Chile got cancelled because of the protests.

BELOW At least someone is having a relaxing day off.

BOTTOM This tour bus looks and feels a bit different from the one I'm used to in Europe, but my first visit to Taiwan was fantastic.

BELOW I had the pleasure of seeing my mural in Kavarna, Bulgaria's rock capital, a few years ago.

TOP In Minsk for my show.

ABOVE These guys took care of me in the Czech Republic on my last Christmas tour. I felt very safe.

BELOW Sometimes on past tours, I've gone among my audience to sing to them – at times, with them.

LEFT I still find it weird to see the huge numbers of fans who come to my signing sessions. This was in Galeria do Rock in Sao Paulo during a tour of Brazil. I met many happy people that day.

BELOW The ancient ruins of Huaca Pucllana Temple in the Miraflores district of Lima, Peru.

BELOW The view on the beautiful day we went to see the statue of Christ the Redeemer.

TOP Don't you have any black bikinis? asked Maria. We felt like tourists at Copacabana beach in Rio. These kinds of moments on tour are the ones that keep me going.

ABOVE Backstage at a German festival and the sun was shining. It really felt like being on the beach.

BELOW We love sightseeing while on tour. This was a cable car trip in Colombia and unfortunately the day was very foggy, so we could not see that much, but it was still worth the visit.

Touring *What Lies Beneath* was a pretty big challenge, but because I had already done that first album tour which had lasted two years, a lot of promoters were already aware of my work. They had heard I was willing to tour with a new album so luckily there was a lot of interest all around the world. That meant I had new markets and countries to visit. I performed in the Ukraine, Costa Rica, Peru and Bolivia, where we got altitude sickness so badly that we had oxygen canisters onstage and in my changing booth – but the fans were so passionate and dedicated. They were waiting when we arrived at the airport and followed us in hired minivans all the way to the city centre.

Estonia was another country I visited for the first time in 2012. I played in Tallinn at Rock Café and returned the following year with *Beauty and the Beat* at Nokia Concert Hall, which was an incredible experience.

Again, the album tour took about two years in total. I had the same lineup as my previous tours, so it was fun to go out on the road with those guys again. I knew it would be hard because of the travelling and the lack of sleep but I could lean on my band and trust them. We were a team and there was a good feeling about it.

We had some amazing experiences too, performing at festivals including Rock On Volga in Russia for over 250,000 people and Rock In Rio (as a guest of local heroes Angra), where everyone went totally crazy. In March 2012, I got my first chance to perform in Costa Rica, where I had taken a month-long holiday with my family in 2005. I've loved the country ever since, having driven around exploring the area, and so was very happy to stay a few days longer with everybody on tour and enjoy the beach. In 2019, I played at the 25th anniversary of Rock Al Parque in Colombia, which was a real honour as well.

I've played to some large crowds but I remember being particularly amazed at the size of the crowd when I played Woodstock in Poland in 2016. It's one of the biggest festivals in Europe and attracts around half a million people. The stage setup was enormous and the audience stretched further than I could see. I wore what I call my wedding gown: a white corset and extravagant skirt, which looked so lovely under the lights. That same year I did Wacken Open Air Festival in Germany and a very special warmup show at Wacken Church two days before. I had a violinist, cellist and pianist with me for the special gig at the church. For the programme we mixed up some classical songs, including my own 'Ave Maria', with metal covers by Avenged Sevenfold, Linkin Park, Megadeth and Rammstein. It was a unique opportunity for me to present a completely different type of programme and everyone loved it. Max Lilja worked really hard on the arrangements for this one-off concert and I would really love to do it again.

That was not the only time that I have performed a classical set for a metal crowd. In 2010, I shocked the Czech Republic's Masters of Rock festival by singing 'Song to the Moon' in Czech with Filharmonie Bohuslava Martinů Zlin. It's a beautiful, melancholic song from the Dvořák opera *Rusalka* and it's a really tough aria. It was such an unbelievable feeling when everyone fell silent. My fans in the Czech Republic have really accepted both sides of me and a lot of that is down to the wonderful work of my promoter there, George Jiri. He's supported me since the beginning of my solo career.

ABOVE My lineup at the acoustic concert in Wacken Church.

BELOW It was overwhelming to sing in front of such a large crowd at Woodstock, Poland.

LEFT On a hot summer night in my backstage container box, trying to get some air.

BELOW Rocking mama.

ABOVE My fans stay faithful and loyal in all conditions. It was raining cats and dogs in Brazil and we were not sure if my show would still take place, but many hours later, it finally did.

LEFT I got a black eye during a festival show in Germany, because some idiot threw a plastic bottle at me. Luckily, I didn't lose my sight.

I LOVE PERFORMING IN THEATRES, EVEN WITH MY ROCK BAND

PREVIOUS PAGE This was a true moment of happiness and pride. We had just finished filming and recording my first live solo rock video at Teatro El Círculo in Rosario, Argentina. The audience was incredible!

LEFT/BELOW LEFT My first live DVD recordings took place in the Teatro el Círculo, Rosario, Argentina. It's just the kind of old opera house I love performing in.

Although I always seek perfection in everything, the perfect concert does not really exist because it depends on so many different factors, both personal and technical. I am living my dream as an artist because I have been able to perform across a whole range of venues and spaces with audiences of all sizes. I love performing in theatres, even with my rock band, and that is probably connected to my first love, classical music. Seated concerts are so peaceful as the audience does not have to fight for a good position during the show and the sound is usually amazing. However, I also love to see my audience pogoing up and down in the circle pit. It is always good to capture these moments and I really enjoy releasing live concerts on an album or on video for my fans to enjoy.

Live recordings are as important to me as the studio albums and I work really hard on them. My first official release was *Act I*, which was filmed with 10 high-definition cameras in March 2012. I had performed at Teatro El Círculo in Rosario, Argentina, the year before and fell in love with it: I thought it would be a beautiful location to film a live video. It is a very important opera house with old-fashioned red velvet seats, multiple-level balconies and very good acoustics. We shot the artwork there with a local photographer, Eugenio Mazzinghi, and there were so many places we could shoot. The main idea behind it was to show the charming location. I named it *Act I* because from the start I wanted to build a concept around my live videos. Acts are used in opera; they appear in the opera libretto, or script book, to separate different scenes and I have used them to represent different stages of my career. I thought it would provide a nice connection to both the venue and my background. There is already a second *Act*, and hopefully one day there will be a third, and so on.

We filmed across two nights because I wanted to have as much material as possible to draw from. On the first night, we performed 'The Phantom of the Opera' with a local metal tenor called Diego Valdez – he has such a huge voice and it was fantastic. We also performed an acoustic set with me singing and then playing piano at the end. It fitted very nicely and it was amazing to see the reactions of the Argentinian audiences – they did not stay in their seats for long and at one point I was thinking, "Uh-oh, I hope we don't get thrown out!"

One thing which was not obvious to everyone is that when we filmed the video, I was five months pregnant with my daughter, Naomi. That was one of the final shows we performed before I had to take a break and only my crew and my family knew that I was expecting. My husband and I were living in Buenos Aires at the time and I remember going to a dressmaker there to get my stage outfits adjusted because I was getting bigger and bigger. Fortunately, no one in the audience seemed to notice so I could keep my secret a while longer.

By the fifth month of my pregnancy, I thought, "That's it, that's as far as I can get." It was just too difficult to jump around in high heels. I was really tired, too. I remember walking around Lisbon in Portugal, up and down the stairs in the old city, I was breathing like an old person because of the pregnancy. Naomi was born on July 27, 2012, just after the touring cycle ended for *What Lies Beneath*. When she was five months old, I began touring again. The first shows were part of my annual Christmas tour of Finland. Before it began, everyone, including my brothers, had been trying to convince me that when I became a mother I would not be able to continue working as I had been. Well, I proved them very wrong!

Naomi came on tour with me for the first four years of her life. She went everywhere in the world with her parents so our life became her life. When I was onstage, Marcelo was taking care of the production, so I had a nanny to take care of Naomi. She was there at the rock concerts and when I was rehearsing with a symphonic orchestra too, but she was the quietest baby, asleep in her travel cot with her big, noise-cancelling headphones on. Nobody even realised a baby was there! It was such an amazing time to be out there with my whole family. We fell into the routine of living on the road with ease, travelling with seven pieces of luggage, and all my crew wanted to play with her. It was important that I carried on working after becoming a mother, and I have learned so much about myself through my daughter. She has seen it all. How many other kids really know what their mother does for work? Mine knows what I do from the minute I wake up until I go to sleep. She embraces all the knowledge she gets from our experiences together and can hopefully use it in later life. When I have to tour alone nowadays it is not easy to leave her behind.

I always say my shows are camera-friendly and *Luna Park Ride* was filmed by my fans. It was so important for me to involve them in the project because without them, I would not be able to do what I do. Estadio Luna Park is in Buenos Aires and was originally used for sports events, mainly boxing, but has been hosting concerts since the 1950s and I loved playing there. The welcome I had there was always amazing, and after my show in 2011, I was cursing myself, saying, "Why did I not film my video here?" That is when I had the idea to ask my fans to send in footage they had filmed

OPPOSITE I am a very proud mum and I will never regret taking my daughter with me on my tours. She has already seen the world and that is probably the best gift I could ever give her.

BELOW I always look for a gym at the hotel we stay in or nearby as I try desperately to maintain good physical fitness when I'm on tour. It has become a very important part of my life on the road.

themselves. We received so much great material it was insane. Some was filmed on proper video cameras and some on phones; personally, I found it an emotional experience to see the concert from a fan's perspective, in the middle of a huge crowd. It was a wonderful idea but very tough to edit everything so that it all made sense. I'm sure most acts would probably cringe at the thought of releasing footage that was not absolutely perfect, but I loved the feeling you could get from it. We included extra footage from festivals shot between 2010 and 2014, and it was nice to be able to show my fans where I have been.

The video ended up complementing *Act I* and being almost a definitive document of the first part of my solo career and I was very happy that we were able to do it that way.

I brought in Tim Palmer to mix the audio and he really did a great job as he always does. I'm a performer and I cannot perform the songs in the same way every night, so whatever happened needs to stay on the audio mix. Of course, the recordings will still be mixed and mastered, but I would never ask anyone to re-record their part after the concert. I do not like the idea of overdubbing live albums and DVDs. Music needs to capture the organic feel of that moment – even if something goes wrong – and I know that's not a common attitude in this industry.

Act II was filmed in two contrasting venues that were deliberately very different from *Act I*. The first part of the video again involved my fans. We ran a competition to win tickets to a very intimate live set at London's Metropolis Studio, which is a very prestigious location where Amy Winehouse's *Back to Black* album was mixed and has also been used by Queen and U2. My performance was filmed on a warm summer's evening in June 2016 and was probably one of the smallest concerts I have ever played: just 20 fans were invited, but it was so nice to do and even nicer to be able to share it with a much larger audience on the video.

ABOVE/OPPOSITE I have always loved Italy for its history and architecture. It was truly wonderful to stroll around the streets of Florence with photographer Tim Tronckoe to take pictures for my second live DVD, *ACT II*.

BELOW Just a little signing to do for my fans.

ABOVE Photographer Paul Harris took shots of me when I was doing an intimate show for a handful of fans in Metropolis Studios, London.

OPPOSITE One of the highlights of my career was playing the piano while up in the air – it felt like the whole world was mine. This was taken at *The Best of Tarja: A Night to Remember* at Circul Metropolitan in Bucharest.

BELOW It is pure pleasure to be in front of the camera lens when my friend, photographer Tim Tronckoe, is behind it. He built a simple set backstage at my *Circus Life* concert in Bucharest and we took photos for the artwork for my *Best of* album.

The second half of the video was shot in a very modern theatre in Milan. Like Teatro El Círculo, it was somewhere I had played before and really wanted to return to, so I took one of my *Shadow* shows there in November 2016. It celebrated a decade of my solo career and involved a huge amount of work. I wanted to experiment and make a live-art video so it would be different from the first live release. This time, the theatre didn't have anything too special to offer in terms of architecture in its walls and spaces, but I still wanted to make it a classy package, so we shot the accompanying photos in Florence. We took the cameras out, literally, onto the streets. The town has so many beautiful buildings and so much history that it perfectly fits the arty theme behind my live releases. It felt like the perfect progression from *Act I*. In the booklet photos I'm wearing a white coat dress that my childhood friend Sirja made me. It was so heavy that I could not use it for live rock performances, so it sat in my wardrobe for years, waiting for me to find the right time to wear it. The whole thing reflects who I am and combines my love of rock and classical both through music and visuals.

One of the most exciting things for me about live recordings is that they often provide the opportunity to showcase different arrangements of songs. It is like breathing new life into them and I really like that. On my next live video, *Circus Life*, filmed in Bucharest, I spent a lot of time working with new arrangements that had never been heard before. For example, there is a super-heavy version of 'Diva' which I love. I have sung these songs so many times and reinventing them gives me a new energy which is really exciting. The Bucharest show was filmed in January 2020 at Circul Metropolitan București, which is a real circus location. The stage was right in the middle of the audience so we could not put up any screens. This helped the audience to completely focus on the music. It was one of two special concerts with an expanded lineup, *The Best of Tarja: A Night to Remember*. The other was held in the Czech

I wanted it to be really special because it celebrates 15 years of my solo career.

Republic in Prague's Smetana Hall at Obecní Dům. We had an amazing lighting designer who has been working with me for 20 years so I knew I could trust him to make a beautiful setup. I wanted it to be really special because it celebrates 15 years of my solo career.

The venue was very challenging technically and I had 16 musicians with me: backing vocalists, a string quartet, a percussionist, two keyboard players, three guitar players, two bass players and a drummer – it was a huge band and we played everything without backing tracks. As amazing as it was onstage, it was just as interesting backstage. There were lots of boxes containing circus costumes and the guys were fooling around, saying, "Hey, let's wear these clown costumes!" I wish I had some funny photos of them but sadly they lost their nerve and never got dressed up. Getting to my warmup room was one big adventure that night, as I had to walk all the way around the arena and past the stables housing real horses. It smelled really funky, but it was such an amazing space to perform in and I am very happy with the finished film.

OPPOSITE PAGE

TOP LEFT This Peruvian bear still belongs to the family today.

TOP RIGHT I love strolling the streets of Rome, so after a long stint travelling in the bus, I had to take some photos.

CENTRE It's a hard job to do a signing alone, but it's a lot of fun with my fans.

BOTTTOM LEFT Can you see my stage in the background? Here I am, shower-fresh, just waiting for the evening to arrive.

BOTTOM RIGHT I love Lebanese food and Pepe's restaurant with its delicious food and service in Biblos, Lebanon, made us all very happy.

*b*efore any show, there is a huge amount of planning that takes place, usually months in advance. I hate repeating my sets so I have them all saved as spreadsheets and I can check which songs I have already performed and where. Of course, some songs must always be performed but I like to surprise people with songs they are not expecting.

I will go through the stage setup with my crew of eight or nine people: two stage technicians, a lighting guy, a front-of-house sound engineer, a monitor engineer, a merchandise guy, my assistant and, in Europe, I have two bus drivers. I need to talk to my lighting engineer and set designer quite early on to check where all the instruments will be positioned. I like to have the drums to the side of me rather than at the back where they'd usually be at a rock concert. I like everyone to have their own space and we all need to be able to see each other in case there are technical problems. Of course, I also need to secure my musicians for the tour, and find out who is available as many of them are session artists who get booked up in advance. You will not see me performing a lot with pyrotechnics. I used to do that with Nightwish but they really affected my voice so I don't use them. I have used flames or white smoke and I like those special effects, but the pyros and explosions are terrible for your throat.

If we are touring in Europe we travel in sleeper coaches called Nightliners. These are large, double-decker buses with a kitchen area, lounge, onboard bathrooms and lots of storage space so we can bring the whole production with us. It is like having my home with me – they even have underfloor heating for when it is cold in the winter. If we are playing in America, South America or Asia, we fly and stay in hotels because of the distance between cities. Either way, the crew takes care of everything and they will start building the stage from very early in the morning.

On the bus, I have my own beautiful room with a bed, a TV and en-suite toilet and shower. My driver changes the sheets almost every day and even lights a scented candle for me. Such luxury on tour! On show days, I will usually have a lie-in but I like to go for a run in the mornings, shower and then eat breakfast or lunch. I also like to be able to say a few words in the local language between songs so once I arrive at my destination I find a local who can help me prepare a few phrases.

TOP This is how my clothes travel when we tour on a bus.

ABOVE Looks like a laundry day on tour.

LEFT My safe haven while on tour. I usually sneak in there right after the shows, have a shower, light a candle, have dinner, read and go to bed.

ABOVE There is always time for sun and coffee. When I was a little girl, I used to travel in a caravan with my parents; now I continue the same way of life on tour.

RIGHT Alex and Kevin panicking while practising a new song I had just decided to add to the acoustic set for the following day – one way to spend the evening on our bus. I love motivating my guys.

ABOVE Susanna Asspera with her bandmates in Buenos Aires before going on stage for her show.

BELOW These are the most important things for making a show happen!

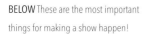

ABOVE I love to change costumes during my shows, and I need some space to do that close to the stage. There is a mirror, kettle, fresh water, ginger, lemon, a towel and my clothes.

LEFT Girls must have fun! My personal assistant Eleonora has saved my butt on several occasions and this is sure to continue.

RIGHT Backstage at a venue – glamour was not part of the deal on that day!

LEFT This is a very common set-up after shows – we hang out together with a nice glass of wine and talk about the show and life before it's time for bed.

BELOW My friends from Angra supported me during my European tour some years ago. It was lovely to listen to these Brazilians (and one Italian) laugh and brighten our days during the tour.

ABOVE It was pretty challenging getting all these people together for the *Best of* shows in the Czech Republic and Romania, but we made it happen.

BELOW Even though it looks like a mess here, the acoustic set in my shows is always a highlight.

After lunch, I usually begin my vocal warm-ups and soundcheck for an hour; my assistant, Eleonora Pedron, will already be waiting for me at the venue and she is in charge of putting up the daily schedules and making sure everyone is where they need to be. She escorts me in and out of the venue and helps with my outfit changes during the show. Before Eleonora came along, my husband used to do all this, but more often than not now he stays at home to look after our daughter.

One of the most important things for me whenever we perform is my changing booth. Sometimes we have to build one; at other times there might be a room that we can use. I love the theatrical nature of live shows and enjoy having outfit changes, but between some songs I have only 45 seconds to change and I am pumped full of adrenaline so Eleonora has to help me. All my clothes are lined up in my booth and she goes: whoosh, whoosh, whoosh! I need her to work super-fast and stay calm because I am a Bitch with a capital B when in my changing booth! If there is something bothering me – perhaps problems with the monitor sound or I've forgotten some lyrics – I complain to Eleonora and she tries to remain calm while putting clothes on me.

Naturally, I have had many wardrobe malfunctions while on stage, including breaking the heel of my shoe and going onstage barefoot, or the zip in my pants getting stuck just as the opening song begins to play – something always happens, but Eleonora fixes everything quickly. She is amazing and I don't know what I would do without her.

When I was a child, my parents would take me to the local theatre to see musicals and I would go backstage and watch the actors putting on their makeup and going through whatever pre-performance rituals they had. Maybe seeing them had an effect on me, because I have my own pre-stage rituals as well. It's really important that I have some alone time before the show, for instance. I like

Christian Kretschmar, keyboard player

"I've been involved with the Schiller project [the German electronic band] for many years. We've always worked with guest artists from many different genres, be it Mike Oldfield, Midge Ure, or even actors who would recite poems live with us on stage. Tarja contributed the beautiful song 'Tired of Being Alone' to the album *Tag und Nacht* in 2006, but unfortunately I didn't meet her in person back then. In 2009, when she was looking for a live pianist/keyboard player, she gave me a call – and the rest is, as they say, history. I arrived at the rehearsal studio for the September tour in 2009, met everybody for the first time, and ever since we've been travelling the world and playing music together.

"As a keyboard player, Tarja's music is the perfect playground. I can unleash the wildest industrial electronic madness, and ten minutes later I can accompany her on the piano for a bombastic rock ballad. Tarja's musical spectrum is as wide as it gets and, as challenging as that sometimes can be, it's just as fulfilling for a musician. Generally, there aren't many opportunities to work with international artists that take you on tour around the world on this level. I've found some real and rare friendships in her band, and I've played for so many people all over the globe – and for that I'm profoundly grateful.

"Since I started working with Tarja, I've been involved in the production of at least some of the songs on all of her albums. It makes a huge difference if you play your own material live on stage, and it's wonderful to know that I can contribute my part in her music and make it last forever on her albums. There are way 'Too Many' favourite songs for me to choose from, but from a strictly live perspective, I love 'Underneath', it's the kind of ballad that every pianist loves. I also love 'Innocence' for the challenge and 'Love To Hate' and 'Medusa' for their attitude.

"It's also hard to just pick one favourite moment from our time together because there are just too many, but I've always loved our acoustic moments onstage. We listen to each other even more closely, and for these 15 minutes in the middle of the set we can get truly lost in playing music together. I even remember a tour back in the day when we actually performed the acoustic set in the middle of the audience – I guess the crew and security didn't like it as much as I did, though! Playing in Hong Kong or in Tokyo, in Manaus or in La Paz with oxygen on stage, or at the Woodstock Festival in Poland in front of almost half a million people, those are moments that no musician will ever forget. But sometimes it's also the private moments after the show that are special, when we sit together with a glass on the tour bus or at the hotel bar after a completely crazy day. Because, after all, we travel the world with friends and do our favourite thing together, that's what makes it all priceless."

RIGHT With the Scorpions. I ran to see them straight after my show in Rock the Coast festival in Spain. It was so great to catch up.

BOTTOM Being the only girl around is the story of my life. These are the people that have supported me through many troubles and miles covered. I have a crew of very talented and dedicated people.

LEFT Klaus Meine's recommended tea is a "must-have" on tour. If I feel that my voice needs a bit of extra care, I enjoy this delicious and healthy drink.

LEFT This is a dream to find backstage.

to close my door and concentrate on me. Preparing my hair and makeup helps me get focused for the show, and I call it "jumping into my beauty box". I also have some herbal infusions that I drink for my voice: either lemon and grated ginger in hot water, or a special tea with liquorice root that Klaus Meine, The Scorpions' singer, recommended to me. Even my daughter loves that tea!

My backstage rider contains mostly healthy stuff, definitely no Jack Daniel's, otherwise I would not still have the voice I do! It's simple: I need a lot of water, fresh berries, peanuts, a fruit basket and espresso coffee. I do appreciate a good wine from time to time so I often ask for a nice Chilean or Argentinian wine, red or white, preferably organic, which I can enjoy after the show. I never drink any alcohol before going onstage, though, otherwise I lose the control in my voice. I know some male opera singers who drink whisky before a show if they need to reach low notes, but sopranos cannot do that. It is far too risky, and we would risk damage to our vocal cords.

On show days, I drink about three litres of pH-balanced water, which is healthier than drinking water from a plastic bottle. My assistant mixes it up using a special alkaline stick. I drink water during the shows, before and after. My voice needs a lot of moisture and I have a portable humidifier on the tour bus so the air does not get too dry.

After the show, I go directly from the stage to the bus for a shower and then I can relax and reflect on my performance while I wait for the guys to finish at the venue. I always eat my final evening meal after the show, usually with a salad or vegetables, maybe with a glass of wine. I eat like a horse on tours and have three proper meals a day because I need a lot of energy. I eat a lot of protein but try not to mix proteins and carbs, otherwise I feel tired.

The bus usually leaves at about two in the morning and we drive through the night to the next town. I do not really sleep well when the bus is moving, although I have got a lot better at this over the years. It is very hard for me to relax and I have suffered many, many years of sleepless nights, but it is so important to try and rest because when the body gets tired, the voice does, too.

If we are flying between shows, we have to be ready to go to the airport very early in the morning. I cannot sleep for more than two or three hours after the show because of all the adrenaline pumping through my body. Flying tours are the hardest and I always try to avoid performing on a flying day because the dry air on aeroplanes is so bad for the voice.

TOP Masi pallopää (Mike) is taking care of the tired girls on tour.

ABOVE CENTRE While on tour – another day at the airport with my guys.

ABOVE This is the normal amount of luggage that travels with me on a long tour. On many occasions, I have felt unsettled, moving back and forth between three houses and touring.

LEFT Just look at our happy faces after my first European tour.

A typical day on tour

11am   Wake up and go for a run.

Midday   Return to the bus, shower and grab something to eat. Begin vocal warm-ups and research some local phrases that I can say onstage.

2pm   Head to the venue for soundcheck. This usually takes around an hour, depending on whether there are any technical issues. I check out the stage and my assistant shows me where my dressing room and changing booth are.

4pm   VIP Meet & Greet. Don't forget the Sharpie!

5pm   Return backstage for a light dinner.

5.30pm   More vocal warm-ups.

6.30pm   Me time! It's time to start transforming myself for the show.

9pm   It's showtime!

11pm   The show ends and I head back to the bus for a shower, some quiet reflection, a light evening meal and a well-deserved glass of wine.

1–2am   Lights out and time for bed!

TOP The daily routine backstage. ANF, a neuro-frequency therapy, has become very important for my performance and recovery as it helps me to sing better.

ABOVE Part of my daily routine on tour is to do some physical exercises at backstage before the show. On this particular day, I must have had pain in my legs.

RIGHT For special shows I have a makeup artist who does my hair and makeup, but on tour, it's all down to me. At this venue, I had good lighting for it.

FAR RIGHT Just look at this beautiful backstage welcome in Brazil! The pillowcases are adorable. The promoter of the show really understands that this mum is missing her child.

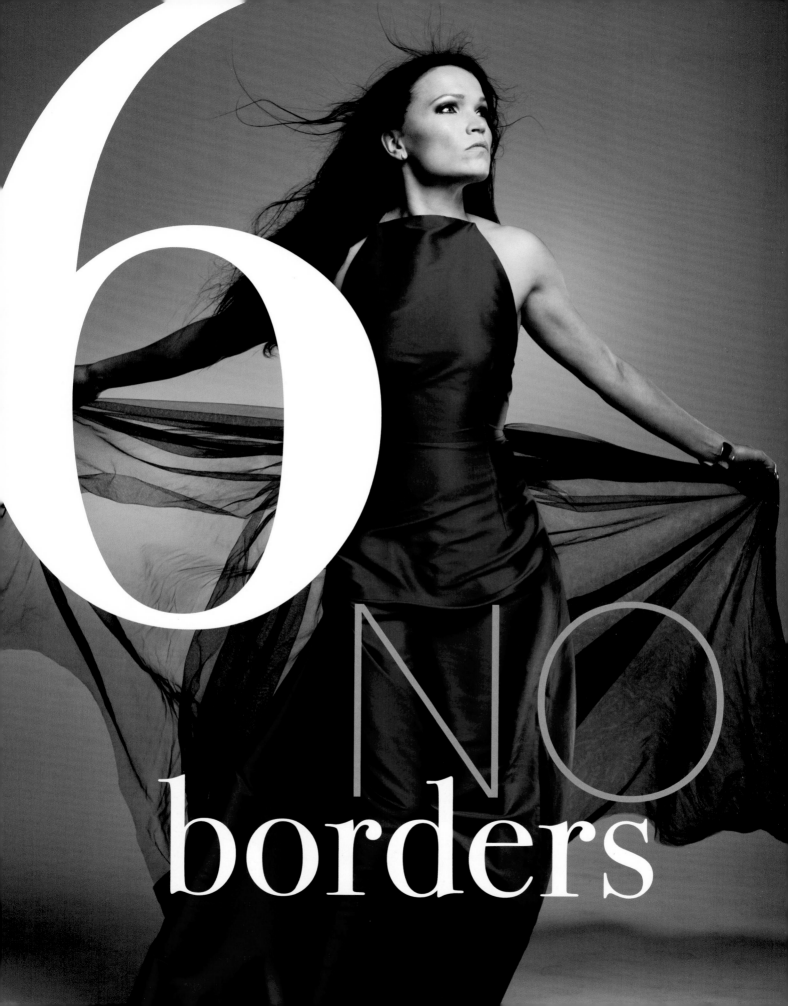

6

NO
borders

ABOVE My university, Hochschule für Musik, in Karlsruhe, Germany. I spent some of the best years of my life in Karlsruhe and made friends for life there. Every now and then when I get to visit the city again, it's like going back in time.

I have always loved the drama of opera and was attracted to the amount of power the voices carried. It is so difficult to explain but when singing opera it feels as though your whole body is vibrating, not just your vocal cords. I will never forget the first time I had that feeling; it made me weep. Although I've been a singer for many years, I still feel there is so much more to learn about my voice and what I can achieve with it. I had always wanted to become a lyrical singer when I was young, before almost accidentally becoming involved in heavy metal. That introduced me to a new world of music that I fell in love with, despite it being a huge challenge to sing. Still though, classical singing keeps me in control of my voice.

When I was studying at the Senior Secondary School of Art and Music in Savonlinna, my voice was already starting to head in an operatic direction. It was my dream to go to Sibelius Academy once I turned 18 but because it is very difficult to get in, I had not dared to apply directly to the singing school as I did not think I was good enough. Instead, I applied to their church music degree course, which included piano and organ playing, conducting choirs and some singing; the syllabus covered so many different bases. To my amazement, I got in after the first audition. I remember receiving my selection letter and running out of my house in the village laughing, running, crying and screaming – I was so happy.

At that time, getting into Sibelius Academy was a really big deal. It is one of the biggest music universities in Europe and the only one in Finland, with campuses in Helsinki and Kuopio. Helsingfors Musikinstitut, as it was then named, was founded in 1882 and renamed in honour of Finnish composer Jean Sibelius, who was a former student. So many famous composers, conductors and musicians have passed through the academy, and my friend who had played organ with me at my church performance a few years earlier was already studying in Kuopio, so I thought it would be a safe environment for me. I also saw the pipe organ as a challenge because not only do you have to play it with your hands moving on different levels of keyboard which, as a pianist, was a completely new skill for me to learn, but you also need to push pedals with your feet.

My studies at Sibelius' Kuopio campus were full-on and I soon discovered *lied* – a German style of singing with a soloist accompanied by a piano – and became really enchanted by it. It is far more intimate than opera because you perform the songs with an accompanist only. While opera is focused on the power of the voice, *lied* requires a more subtle performance in which you tell a story through lyrics, which can be difficult to sing well.

Not long after I had begun my studies at Sibelius, I was invited to sing on the demo of a new acoustic project. This project, which later became Nightwish, evolved away from the initial acoustic approach and into heavy metal. As the band grew and we started releasing albums and touring, I had to juggle everything with my studies, which was extremely hard. I was trying to fight jet lag during my classes, and it was very demanding, but I wanted to do it. My teachers and my singing coach were encouraging me to pursue my classical singing and, with their support, I decided to transfer to the vocal music degree, which was taught at the Helsinki campus. I thought it would be easier to switch courses because I was already an undergraduate student at the academy, but I was wrong. I remember standing in front of the board to apply and they said to me, "What are you doing here when you are touring with this heavy metal band of yours?"

That was when I realised how much prejudice exists in the world of classical singing. They could not understand what I did, and they would not accept me on the merit of my talent; it was as though I had a stamp on my forehead. I was too well-known in Finland by then and it felt claustrophobic to stay there. By this point, I had already been at Sibelius for four years and wanted to continue with my singing studies. I was already having success with the band and wanted to keep on doing that, but I also wanted to become a successful classical singer one day. *Lied* is my passion, it is part of me, and I wanted to keep on singing it, but I never wanted to say goodbye to rock 'n' roll. So, I started to look for universities in Europe, particularly in Germany, because I was very familiar with the language as I had been learning it since primary school and I had also studied at the Goethe Institute of Helsinki.

Marcelo (who I was not yet married to) hired a rental car and together we visited several universities in Germany. When I saw the romantic pink castle with grey turrets of Hochschule für Musik in Karlsruhe as we drove towards it, I was, like, "Wow! This is an amazing campus!" It was beautiful and inspiring, so when I found out about the professors who taught there I started dreaming about getting in. There was a particular professor, mezzo-soprano Mitsuko Shirai, who I really wanted to tutor me, and when I discovered that she was just as enthusiastic for me to be her student I knew that it was the place for me, and I studied under her from 2000 to 2002.

Studying there was a very different experience compared to Sibelius. At Karlsruhe, I studied seven days a week in German with Mitsuko. She had enjoyed a career as a performer and artist before she started teaching, and although I came to her classes thinking that I knew something about singing, after the first lesson I felt like I knew nothing at all. It was a very tough course. Every week I had to learn new songs by heart and practise them with the pianist, as well as studying all the other subjects. It was a technical rollercoaster but, thanks to Mitsuko, my voice is now so flexible. She taught me so much and her training has become the backbone of my singing career. After she helped me to open my heart, it became fun and I began to have more trust in myself and in what I was doing.

While in Karlsruhe I shared a house on campus with some of the other singers and we would rehearse there. It was an old, creaking building nicknamed the 'Hell House' because any time you passed by, all you could hear was operatic singing, which sounded like a choir in hell. It was super-hot in the summer and there was no air conditioning, so all the windows were kept open. Our poor neighbours!

When I was 18, my teacher had warned me against opera, out of fear that it would damage my vocal cords – and she was right. There were singers of my age at Karlsruhe who had begun working professionally immediately after their studies and had ended up having huge problems with their voices. Fortunately, I didn't have those problems. It was continually drilled into us how important it was for everyone to learn how to use their voice safely. Your voice is like a muscle: just as you cannot run a marathon without training, so it is with lyrical singing. Your body should remain elastic otherwise your voice comes out too hard and it doesn't vibrate naturally, so you have to maintain suppleness. I know I have been very lucky that rock 'n' roll singing hasn't damaged my voice over the years.

I loved my time in Karlsruhe but quit my course in late 2002 when my mother became very ill with cancer, and I felt I had to be with her. There was only one concert that I needed to perform in order to get my diploma, but I felt my mother needed me more than I needed that piece of paper on my wall. I had already proven many times that I was capable of playing concerts, so I

ABOVE Mitsuko Shirai, my singing teacher at Hochschule für Musik, Karlsruhe. She was incredibly supportive and understanding, even though I was constantly away on tours and busy with other engagements, she was always there for me.

BELOW The singers' 'Hell House' at the university in Karlsruhe. This photo was taken during my last rock tour in Germany.

said goodbye to Germany and that was the end of my formal studies. Those two-and-a-half years of my life in Karlsruhe were amazing, though, and I learned so much about singing and *lied*. It was a memorable time that helped give me the confidence to combine my rock career with classical projects. The first of which was the *lied* group Noche Escandinava, which translates as a 'Scandinavian Night'. I formed the group in 2002 with some of my classmates from Karlsruhe. At that time, I was already known as a rock singer, and I was starting to become known in South America too, so I knew that I could tour there, on a small scale. I thought it would be amazing to present a programme of Nordic and Scandinavian music to Latin American people, and my friends – Norwegian singer Ingvild Storhaug, the Finn Marjut Paavilainen and Japanese pianist Izumi Kawakatsu (who was working closely with all of us in class and would later play piano on some of my albums) – loved the idea. We performed the first concerts in Chile and Argentina, choosing a Spanish name for the events for these Spanish-speaking countries. Most of the people coming to see us were rock fans, but we had such fabulous feedback and it was a really great experience.

Performing these shows made me feel completely naked, though. There were no microphones, just sung poetry and harmony and the piano. I was still studying at this point of course, and so I was very self-critical. (I still get more nervous about performing classical music onstage than I ever do before rock shows.) We toured twice more as Noche Escandinava, although with different lineups. In 2004, the Finnish baritone Juha Koskela joined us and we took a completely

ABOVE My Karlsruhe gang. Here we are practising the stage act for first Noche Escandinava concerts. I love these girls and I miss them dearly.

LEFT Our second round with Noche Escandinava in Teatro Margarita Xirgu in Buenos Aires, Argentina. I remember being incredibly nervous that night, but the Argentinean audience was amazing and made it a wonderful evening.

ABOVE Outside the National Museum of Art of Romania. The concert posters were very impressive!

RIGHT Marjut, meow. We sang 'Duetto buffo di due gatti' (the cats' duet) by Rossini together and made people laugh in our concerts. Thanks for the headbands, Naomi.

OVERLEAF After 14 years, Noche Escandinava made a comeback with a performance in Buenos Aires. We have all spread our wings in the music world, but nothing beats performing with friends who share my love of classical tunes.

PERFORMING
THESE SHOWS
MADE ME FEEL
COMPLETELY NAKED

TOP With my "Guest of Honour" plate and certification from the city of Buenos Aires. I lived there for almost 10 years and the place will always have a very special place in my heart.

ABOVE Crossover concert in Finland. My dress is by Finnish dress designer, Jukka Rintala.

Finnish programme to Romania, Brazil, Argentina and Chile. We got together to perform again in 2018 and it was hugely enjoyable to meet up with people I had studied with almost 20 years previously. We shared some incredible memories and laughed a lot – it was such a fun tour, and I was declared "Guest of Honour" of the city of Buenos Aires! That was a strange experience because the representatives of the government had been at my concert before I received that accolade, which is normally given to very important artists such as Sting, Lady Gaga, Tom Cruise, Paul McCartney, Al Pacino or José Carreras, among others. It was such a big deal to me that they saw me as somebody worthy of such respect.

My next classical project began a few years later, in 2006. I was invited to perform at a one-off concert with the organist Kalevi Kiviniemi at the Church of the Cross in Lahti, Finland. Kalevi is one of the top organists in the world and the concert was organised as part of the Lahti Organ Festival, but we decided to make the programme a little crazier by also bringing in percussionist Markku Krohn and guitarist Marzi Nyman. We performed cover versions of songs by Nirvana and Deep Purple and the audience went totally nuts – in a good way! We had such an amazing time – with the crowd giving us standing ovations – but the press did not seem to understand it at all. We all felt fantastic after that concert and wanted to make a studio album one day, but we were all so busy with our other projects that several years passed before we were able to get together again. The next time was for another concert.

In 2009, during a break on the *Storm* tour, we reunited as Harus – the name is a Finnish word for the metal cables that support the mast of a ship. It implies balance and strength and represents the four pillars, the four musicians, that support the music, which we felt was perfect. We organised a Christmas tour and recorded our concert at Sibelius Hall in Lahti. At the time it was the only venue in Finland that had an organ so that was one of the reasons we used it. Another was the acoustics: we knew how good it sounded as we had each played there before.

The set was based on Finnish Christmas songs with a couple of versions of 'Ave Maria', including mine. It was a very Finnish programme but with completely different arrangements. Many people think of Finland as a very accepting country when it comes to heavy metal music – after all, we did enter Lordi into

the Eurovision Song Contest – but when it came to classical music, at that time they were not so open-minded. Throughout my life I have pushed boundaries and shaken things up, and I love doing it. When the Harus recording, *In Concert – Live At Sibelius Hall,* was finally released in 2011, many people thought I was giving up on metal, which was not the case at all! Had they never heard my classical singing before?

The Harus album was my first project for earMUSIC. My contract at Universal was up and I was looking for a record label that would not only release my rock albums but my other projects, too. The label boss, Max Vaccaro, really saw my potential and understood what I wanted to achieve – we've been working together ever since and he's become a good friend to Marcelo and me.

It was earMUSIC that released my first proper classical solo record, *Ave Maria – En Plein Air,* in 2015, and by then people had started to understand what I was about. That album helped me to find the harmony and balance between classical and rock and it is such a blessing that I can do both. It took me a long time to record, partly because I was busy with everything else, but also because I didn't have the guts to do it before. I didn't think I was capable of recording a proper classical album – but I am happy to have proved myself wrong.

ABOVE During filming and recording a Harus concert in Lahti Sibelius Hall, Finland.

BELOW From left: Organist Kalevi Kiviniemi, guitarist Marzi Nyman and percussionist Markku Krohn. I had the pleasure of playing several shows and touring with this group of very talented musicians from Finland. Each concert was unique.

Max Vaccaro, General Manager, earMUSIC

"Tarja is a really important artist in the earMUSIC catalogue because, unlike so many others, she's a role model and inspires fans all over the world. As a label, we've always had that immediate and direct feedback from her fans, who've told us how much her albums have meant to them. It's very challenging to work with an artist who has achieved so much in the past and touched so many people with her previous band and solo albums. There's a big responsibility to be creative and quick in order to continue the path of her success.

"Tarja's first release on earMUSIC was *Tarja Turunen & Harus – In Concert Live At Sibelius Hall*. This was a chance for us to get to know each other personally and professionally. It was followed by *Act I*, which was a real success and entered the German album charts at No.3. It quickly gained the fans' appreciation and was released in many different formats. With this live release, Tarja symbolically turned the page after her first two studio albums and started the collaboration with us that is still ongoing.

"I have some great memories of watching her fans lining up to see her in Milan, my home town; her headlining the show at Wacken; a show at Metropolis Studio in London for only 20 fans (which is included in the *ACT II* box set). The days we spent together in London filming the video for 'Tears in Rain' and many other occasions where we shared great food, talked about music (and everything else), along with her manager and husband Marcelo, who over the years has grown to be a very good friend.

"Every one of Tarja's releases is special to me: the challenges we faced, the conversations we had about the artwork, the hope and enthusiasm the day before each release. Musically speaking, I really like *In the Raw* because, as the title suggests, the production and the songwriting valued the spontaneity and not the artificial production of – in my opinion – too many heavy rock/metal albums of today. The album has a beautiful, natural sound, it's a great heavy-rock album with a lot of strong songs. *The Shadow Self* also includes some of my favourite songs, like the epic finale 'Too Many'.

"I truly admire Tarja's determination and her attention to detail, which goes from the artwork of a concert poster, or a digital single, to the full concept of a new studio album. Most of all, I admire the fact that she's never taken the easy way of repeating what she's done before. Many artists in a similar position would have pursued a solo career that was an extension of their original band, but she chose not to. Tarja respects her fans; she's very grateful for their support and she shows it by releasing music that she really believes in; music that reflects what her tastes and interests are at the time she's recording. The proof is the fact that she includes Nightwish songs in her show when she thinks they make sense with the rest of the music, and not because she feels obliged to.

"On a personal level, I respect the fact that Tarja maintains her professional motivation, not at the expense of her family life, and not at the expense of renewing her passions outside the heavy rock world, whether that's music, movies or books."

Over the years, Kalevi Kiviniemi had performed and recorded many versions of 'Ave Maria', and he was always pushing me, telling me, "Come on, you should do an 'Ave Maria' album. Your voice is getting better." Marta, my singing teacher in Buenos Aires, was also supportive of my plan to release a classical album. Bravely, I took the challenge to record the album with Kalevi and started doing my research. 'Ave Maria' is a Catholic prayer and I was blown away by the fact there are more than 4,000 versions of it by all sorts of composers. Maybe you know of one or two, but I knew quite a few because I had already sung several – two of them are on my *Harus* album and I recorded Schubert's version for *Henkäys Ikuisuudesta*. I had also composed my own 'Ave Maria', a live version of which is on the album. Because I was doing the Christmas concerts every year, I thought I would write one in Buenos Aires with my piano. I was really inspired after listening to an album by the film composer Craig Armstrong called *Piano Works* and it only took me a few minutes to come up with it. It was the quickest song I'd ever written.

I contacted a guy in America who runs an 'Ave Maria' webpage and there's even an appreciation society for them. I learned so much and went through so many scores to find the versions that would be best for my voice.

Some of the songs I chose for the final tracklisting were my favourite 'Ave Maria's or ones I had already performed, while others were completely new to me. One of the most challenging ones was by the Argentinian tango composer Astor Piazzolla. He was a true rule-breaker and his piece has a very wide-ranging vocal melody, but I love it because it connects me to Argentina and to Marta. Another very important one was written by Pietro Mascagni and is taken from *Cavalleria Rusticana* – it's the only one from opera. I performed it as part of an opera choir when I was 18.

Although I'm not a Catholic or a religious person, I have always felt that churches are the best places to perform 'Ave Maria', so I chose to record the album at Lakeuden Risti, a Lutheran church in Seinäjoki, Finland. This was in 2011 and I flew my vocal coach over from Buenos Aires so we could prepare my voice for the recordings. I was still a nervous wreck on recording days, though. The songs were recorded without any amplification, live in the church, as if for an audience – except there was none. The acoustics are amazing. Lakeuden Risti was designed by one of Finland's most famous architects, Alvar Aalto. It has a cathedral-style ceiling and an organ layout on the balcony. I had sung there before and knew how spectacular Kalevi would find the organ. We were joined for the recording by harpist Kirsi Kiviharju and cellist Marius Järvi.

We spent two days recording at the church and listened to the playback straight away. I was super-critical, but it was a once-in-a-lifetime experience. I later toured the album in Switzerland, Bulgaria, Finland and the Czech Republic with a different lineup. I really enjoy the more intimate setting of quartet shows; I feel like my voice can be appreciated in its purest sense. We played at Ateneul Român, which is one of Bucharest's most historic sites. Opened in 1888, it is a circular, neoclassical building with the most unbelievable colours inside; we put up very simple, beautiful lights for our Christmas concert and the whole place looked magical. It's always a dream to be able to play on these stages.

ABOVE LEFT Lakeuden Risti, Cross of the Plains church in Seinäjoki, Finland. I enjoyed every second of recording my album there.

ABOVE Mixing, editing and mastering process with Mika Koivusalo. Mika has worked on the recordings of several lyrical singers, and has an accurate ear for classical music, but his support and kindness during the production of my *Ave Maria* album was amazing. I really enjoyed working with him.

LEFT How much I love listening to my voice.

BELOW Organist Kalevi Kiviniemi preparing to record my 'Ave Maria' composition.

ABOVE What an honour it was to perform an *Ave Maria* concert in The Great Hall of Moscow State Conservatory in Russia.

LEFT It's amazing the healing my soul gets during my concerts – thanks to my incredible audiences.

There are two other fantasy venues I would love to play one day. The first is The Royal Albert Hall in London where I saw an amazing live orchestral performance of the *Lord of the Rings* soundtrack by the Royal Philharmonic Orchestra. The other is the Teatro Colón, the main opera house in Buenos Aires, Argentina, where my then-future-husband proposed to me during a performance of Bellini's *Norma*. It is one of those old theatres with beautiful velvet curtains and seats, and it takes your breath away when you walk in.

When I perform my classical projects, the halls are packed. I have loads more people coming to these performances than to my rock shows, but I also have many classical fans come and see me at rock concerts, too. People are looking for new experiences and my fans are very, very loyal. I have people who've been following me since 1996 and they are still coming to my shows. It is wonderful to look out over the audience and see so many different people; young, old, in suits or heavy metal T-shirts – there are no boundaries.

The seeds of my unique musical style were sown by accident. The very first demo I recorded with Nightwish had acoustic guitars but it became very clear that my voice was too powerful for that type of music and so the idea of blending heavy metal with classical singing was born. Back in 1996, I was not really that familiar with the heavy metal scene and I did not know about any of the other bands who were following a similar path around this time. My voice changed dramatically over the first few years of lyrical training and that transformation took me on a journey towards developing my own sound as a solo artist.

It is so important to me to allow space for every element in my songs. I want to hear all the beautiful colours of the orchestra, for the guitars to be as heavy as possible, and I want my vocals to be at the forefront of the mix so the listener can really appreciate them. This is a very unusual way of doing things but I have always broken the boundaries in the worlds of both classical music and metal.

It has never once occurred to me to give up rock although I have been asked so many times: "Which one would you choose?" The truth is, I could never pick one over the other. Classical music and metal complete me, and I would become a very miserable person if I was only singing classical music. It would take away my freedom to express myself, to write songs and to get out there to perform them to my audiences. I live for that – but I breathe for classical singing, too, and classical music soothes my soul. I would not be happy if I had to lose one of these from my life.

Beauty and the Beat, which I performed live with my former drummer Mike Terrana in 2013, was a project that allowed me to demonstrate my passion for both musical styles in the same show. Mike and I first met on my first European tour with Nightwish when he was playing with Rage. I loved listening to his drums; I think I was the only person from the band who was always standing at the back of the venue listening to his solos. When I was planning the tour lineup for *My Winter Storm,* I called him and asked, "Do you remember me?" Straight away, he said he would do it.

OPPOSITE Don't you just love the purple of the Congress Centre of Zlin in the Czech Republic? We did a photo session with Mike Terrana for the artwork of our *Beauty and the Beat* live DVD there.

"Classical music and metal complete me.

Mike was part of my studio and live band when we started this project. I had already performed several times with symphonic orchestras and had enjoyed the experience, but Mike had never done this before. He had, however, released a classical album – 2010's *Classics for the New World* – on which he played drums with an orchestral arrangement, but using keyboards rather than a full orchestra. I enjoyed his album because it was different and I remember discussing it with him on the tour bus. He told me it would be a dream come true for him to perform with a symphonic orchestra and I said, "OK, should we do a project together with vocals, drums and orchestra?" I have never been afraid of doing new things.

ABOVE Rehearsals with conductor Levon Manukyan for the first concert of *Beauty and the Beat* in Plovdiv, Bulgaria.

OPPOSITE *Beauty and the Beat* concert in the stunning Saint Petersburg Philharmonia, Russia

We were fooling around on the tour bus trying to come up with a title in the vein of *Beauty and the Beast*, and Mike naturally came up with *Beauty and the Beat* – as in a drum beat. It was a funny name and we wanted to make an entertaining programme that also had a serious side, with classical music accompanying it. The promoters took a while to understand the concept because this sort of thing had not been done before. We had to explain it to them very carefully, and in the end it was a really successful project. It was different from anything I had done before but it was very enjoyable and I even ended up playing drums on a cover of 'In Other Words', an old song which was made famous by Frank Sinatra under the title 'Fly Me To The Moon'. I knew Mike loved Sinatra and I wanted him to sing the song. I grew up with my brother playing the drums every day at home, so I knew the basic beats, but the way Mike Terrana hits drums is NOT the way I hit them!

I chose the classical songs based on the repertoire I had been performing for years along with some new ones I selected to challenge myself. Everything needed to be rearranged, especially for the drums. The rock selection was more of a joint effort. Mike was already performing some Led Zeppelin at his drum clinics, and I came up with the idea of the 'Led Zeppelin Medley' after watching the movie *Shrek* with my daughter. I heard 'Kashmir' sung by a soprano and thought, "I need to do that!"

I love Queen and chose 'You Take My Breath Away', which was originally based on the Japanese pentatonic scale. To make it something new and special, I performed it a cappella with a choir. 'Witch-Hunt' was one of my own, unreleased songs that I performed with the orchestra and everyone loved it. Eventually it was released on *The Brightest Void*. 'Swanheart' was an old Nightwish song performed in a beautiful arrangement with the orchestra, the idea being to push boundaries and surprise people.

I have never been afraid
of doing new things.

We recorded a live album and video at Kongresové Centrum (Prague Congress Centre) in the Czech Republic. We had more than 70 instrumentalists onstage – but that was not the only challenge. Mike wanted to present the same drum set he uses in his rock shows, which is huge, so we needed to use Plexiglass to dampen down the huge amount of decibels it produced, otherwise the orchestra musicians would not have been able to hear themselves play. It was such an unusual experience for everyone as Mike was providing the beat for an orchestra who had probably never worked with a rock drummer before. Likewise, it was the first time Mike had ever worked with an orchestra and he did not realise that the players would often get up to take a break during the set if they did not have a part coming up. That caused a few misunderstandings, but I managed to smooth things over.

BELOW In Zlin we filmed and recorded a live video of *Beauty and the Beat.*

That was not the only technical issue, however. I remember when we arrived in Peru and discovered that the orchestra had not practised any of the set. It's common to only have one rehearsal before the show, but they misunderstood the whole concept and some of the musicians were missing altogether. We got halfway through the warmup and I told Marcelo that we would have to cancel the concert. It was such a struggle but in the end, we cut the programme in half and gave a shorter performance. I could not disappoint all the fans who had turned up.

The set was incredibly demanding vocally because it starts from classical and then goes through Led Zeppelin and Queen and into my own songs.

Despite these logistical obstacles we played some pretty amazing concerts as part of this project. This tour gave me the chance to visit Musiikkitalo in Helsinki. It has a central stage, where the audience surrounds you, and it's quite a challenge to work out where to put the choir and orchestra for the best sound experience, especially when you have a drummer hitting hard as well! My dad came to this show and he loved it.

Although *Beauty and the Beat* was conceived as a one-off project, it didn't quite run its full course. The project came to an abrupt end because Mike Terrana and I couldn't agree on how to continue working together, but I would love to do more concerts like it in future. The set was incredibly demanding vocally because it starts from classical and then goes through Led Zeppelin and Queen and into my own songs, which each require completely different vocal styles. Still, I would happily put myself through it all again.

I am really looking forward to doing another classical album and my wish is to one day record at least one *lied* album. I would like to go back and work closely with a piano on a Finnish *lied* album before I dare to enter the German world of *lied*, though. I have begun going through scores of Finnish composers and think that would be a fantastic challenge. Maybe one day it will happen. My life is filled with challenges – I embrace them. I also love being able to balance classical and rock music. It is such a blessing that I can continue to do both.

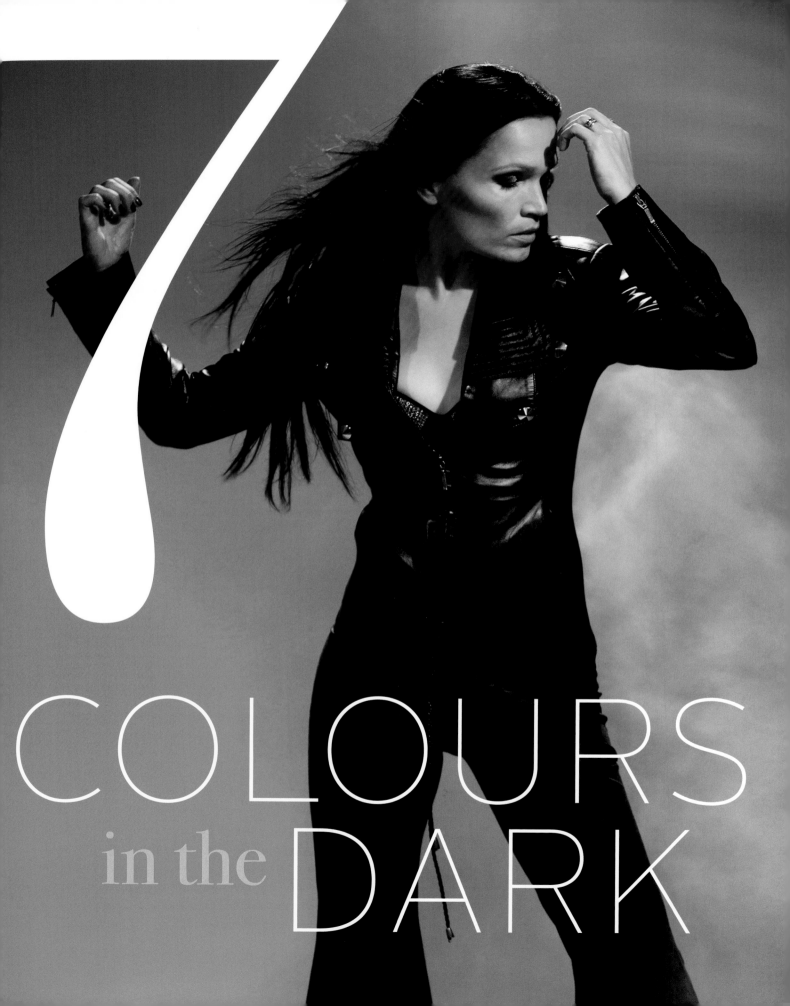

7
COLOURS
in the DARK

Marcelo and I had always planned to start a family and so all my creative work had to be woven around that. That meant I had to begin work on *Colours in the Dark* even earlier than usual and that is why we ended up shooting the cover images before I had even recorded the music. At the time, I was at the beginning of my pregnancy, but I already had a very clear picture of the album, which I knew was going to be about colours. The working title for the album was *Black*, because black absorbs all colours and they are still present inside it. It felt like a very strong concept, but the title was not quite right; I wanted something more, well, colourful, and eventually chose *Colours in the Dark*. The idea was that when you turn the lights off in a colourful room, you know the colours are still there even if you cannot see them, just as you do not always see a person's true colours when you first meet them. It took the theme I had begun to explore on *What Lies Beneath* a little bit further.

The most important songs for the album were written in Antigua. Every time I had a break from my tour, I would go there and write songs with Mattias and Anders, Johnny Andrews and my friend Angela. The island makes me feel so alive, it is magical and I am inspired by the ocean and the idea of solitude, being far away from everything. My daily life is very hectic, and I am surrounded by so many people all the time that it is good to be able to take some time out and rest. When I am on the island, I do not need to stress about what I am doing today or tomorrow, I can just be with my own thoughts.

Antigua has 365 beaches – one for every day of the year – and it is possible to walk in the white sands along the shoreline without encountering anyone. You are surrounded by swaying palm trees, lush, green rainforest, beautiful shells and that powerful ocean: on the Atlantic side it crashes against the rocks and makes a huge, majestic noise, but on the Caribbean side, it is entirely peaceful and you can barely hear the waves. I love to listen to all the sounds of the animals that live on the island, too. The colibri birds are my favourite: they are tiny hummingbirds that appear every morning. They are so beautiful, and flap their wings so fast you barely see more than a flash of colour as they zip by.

If you look out over the horizon, you can see the island of Montserrat, which is where The Beatles' producer George Martin set up AIR recording studio. That's where some of my favourite artists – Michael Jackson, Paul McCartney and Sting – have recorded albums. The island was struck by Hurricane Hugo in 1989 and the Soufrière Hills volcano erupted six years later, which destroyed the city. The volcano is still surrounded by clouds and is a reminder of how dangerous nature can be and how all its colours can be extinguished in an instant by one cloud of darkness and the grey ash that covers everything after.

OPPOSITE In Antigua I love to ride my bike, and also swim in the turquoise water that is just so inviting.

BELOW Looking for inspiration. This photo was taken from our friend Torsten's boat on our first visit to Antigua. That boat ride made me fall in love with the island – you can really appreciate it from the sea.

66

I love to
listen to
all the
sounds of
the animals
that live on
the island.

There were so many issues I wanted to explore on *Colours in the Dark*, some very serious and others less so. Although Antigua's vibrancy and diversity inspired *Colours in the Dark*, there is no connecting storyline as such on the album. Of course, there is always darkness in everything I do and I cannot get away from it, but on this album, I wanted to experiment with new ideas and instruments: for example, instrumentalists playing weird and spooky-sounding instruments such as the glass harmonica and duduk, an Armenian woodwind instrument that I first heard on Peter Gabriel's *Passion* album. I also wanted to be more progressive with my songwriting. Little by little, I was starting to get out of my comfort zone, to break the rules that had been applied to my previous albums and try things that I had never done before. I felt more confident, more relaxed and it was a great experience. Around this time, I was listening to a lot of Peter Gabriel's solo work, as well as darker, more progressive pop bands such as The Cure and Tears For Fears. I was definitely listening more to old music than new and also some of Craig Armstrong's soundtracks – such as *Love Actually* (2003) and *The Great Gatsby* (2013).

TOP I am usually pretty nervous about recording the piano for my albums, but I still do it, because I enjoy playing so much. It is, after all, the instrument I compose with. Here I am recording tracks for *Colours in the Dark* in Panda Studios in Buenos Aires.

ABOVE A month before I exploded… or, in other words, became a mum. We were working with Alex on the guitar recordings for *Colours in the Dark* in El Pie Studios in Buenos Aires.

RIGHT Glamorous way to record vocals, right? In Antigua, we couldn't get a better desk or control room for Torsten to do his work.

We started recording the first songs in Buenos Aires a month before Naomi, my daughter, was born – just drums, guitar and me and my huge belly! I was having the best time. I was happy and healthy, and perhaps in some way this colourful album was connected to my joy about becoming a mother. Three months after Naomi was born, I was back recording vocals for the album and it was brilliant. I loved having her around and we were one big, happy family.

Naomi also made her very first guest appearance on the album with 'Lucid Dreamer'. It is a very experimental song about people who are able to control their dreams. Marcelo can do that; he can create incredible stories and fight monsters, build castles – whatever he wants to do. If he has a nightmare, he can have fun with it. The song is really about freedom and letting yourself go. When we were writing it in Antigua, Naomi was screaming and we nicknamed her "the seagull", but when I recorded my first vocals, she was so quiet. I think she had heard so much music in my belly that it soothed and calmed her no matter how loud it was. One day, when she was playing, Marcelo decided to record her and then we found a song where we could use our daughter's voice for the first time.

There are two love songs on the album, 'Until Silence', which I wrote with Marko Saaresto, Olli Tukiainen and Markus Kaarlonen from the Finnish band Poets of the Fall; and 'Deliverance', which I wrote with Jim, Mattias and Anders. I said to Jim, "You've been doing so much with the arrangements, would you like to have a song on the album?" He took up the challenge. It is a more progressive, symphonic song than anything I had done before. As always, the music came to me first and it felt like a relationship: there is a battle and then calm again; a battle and then calm. It is like any relationship you can think of, emotionally. It was a nice idea to write a love song but not a cheesy one – I never want to go there.

LEFT Do you see the little purple heart under Naomi's name? That was my first tattoo, but I didn't like it because it felt like a stamp on my leg, so I decided to add Finnish flowers – peonies and violets – to it.

BELOW We wrote 'Until Silence' with Marko Saaresto and the rest of Poets of the Fall guys.

'500 Letters' is more serious; it was written (with Johnny) about a stalker of mine and looks at what happens when adoration escalates to a very sick level of fanaticism. This guy in Finland started sending me letters to my home address every two weeks and they were full of violence and sex. It was horrible and I needed to get this out of my system, which I did in this song. I eventually found out that the author was a patient at a mental health facility and the nurses treating him were shocked because they had no idea what had been going on. When they went to his apartment, they found more than 500 letters addressed to me saved in a box. I had to get the police involved in the end and the letters stopped, but then Marcelo started getting calls from an unknown number on his phone. The guy just kept repeating my name; he was very unwell. Eventually, the calls stopped, and we have not heard from him for a number of years now. Unfortunately, that kind of thing has occurred repeatedly throughout my career. It is scary because I meet a lot of people wherever I go, and I treat everyone the same but there are some who cannot just accept the smile, hug or simple kindness and they become infatuated. It was very inspiring for me to write about obsession and it is a theme I explored again on *The Shadow Self* in 'Love To Hate' (written with Erik Nyholm and Angela).

'Victim of Ritual' (written with Mattias and Anders) is about getting away from the everyday. We Finns try to do everything as perfectly as possible and we live our lives without realising we have not lived. We want our children to be perfect, our work to be perfect and for everyone around to think we are perfect, but we keep our rituals away from the public eye. It is always so nice to see how my fans have received this message and when I perform this song, they have coloured powder on their faces, just like I have on the album's cover artwork, because we all, one way or another, are victims of our rituals. Hopefully, we can rid ourselves of them but as you get older you start to understand yourself better. On 'Mystique Voyage', I wanted

ABOVE I wanted to meet the person behind the beautiful 'Sing for Me' song, and after Erik Nyholm and I met we ended up writing more songs together in his studio in Finland. Here, we were sketching out 'Love to Hate', but it took me a few years to come back to it and finish it on my own.

OPPOSITE I bet you won't believe this, but I was recording vocals while my daughter was awake and listening to my voice. She had got used to hearing music in my belly already, so when she was born, she was a super-relaxed and quiet baby.

BELOW Shooting a scene from the 'Victim of Ritual' video in Berlin with director Florian Kaltenbach. That day was a long one and I remember shooting ended at about 5am. It all was worth it, though.

to take the plunge and write in Spanish because it is a beautiful language. When I first moved to Buenos Aires, I didn't dare talk too much in Spanish, but the longer I was there, the more I understood. The lyrics are about my life and it is a very personal song in every way: about believing in your dreams, fighting for them and going forward with them. As I say in the opening lines: "Welcome to my mystique voyage… Welcome to my world!" When I wrote it, Argentina had become a very important part of my life, it was where I had found a new home and had been very much welcomed there, so this track reflects my gratitude for that.

On every album, I have tried to write a fantasy story and 'Medusa' is the one on *Colours*. It has a strange, movie vibe and I wrote the lyrics with Angela in the Caribbean and the music with Bart Hendrickson. When I was recording the vocals, I knew it had to be a duet because it had a depth that I couldn't develop on my own. I remembered Tim Palmer telling me about a band he was working with called Blue October and I really loved the voice of the singer, Justin Furstenfeld; he expresses so much emotion that it brings me to tears. I asked Tim if he would ask Justin for me and he agreed to do it. I was so happy to have him on this album – he is one of those few singers who can deliver emotion. He is a real storyteller.

ABOVE I met Bart Hendrickson on my first visit to Remote Control Productions in LA, but we didn't write any songs together. He is a rocker, drummer and movie-score composer, so his knowledge, experience and his beautiful character meant we understood each other really well. We have written some of the most progressive, weird and dark songs together, including 'Medusa', 'Crimson Deep' and 'Spirits of the Sea'.

RIGHT It is always exciting to watch the audience coming in before my shows.

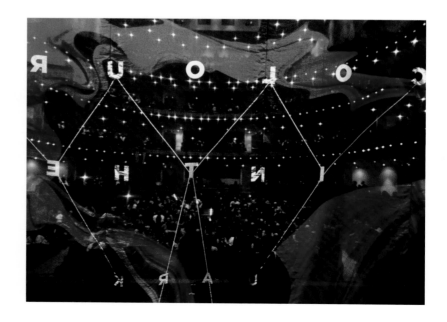

Tim Palmer, mixing

"I love the different styles that Tarja's music embraces; she'll combine electronica with the strength of the rock music, and then Jim Dooley, who does her arrangements, will add in a vast sonic soundscape. *In the Raw* was more stripped down, but I really liked that combination, and sitting right on top of it is Tarja with her massive vocals. She can go from a whisper through to full-on rock goddess. I love the way that Tarja interprets songs and the way she emotes with her vocal performance. I've been very fortunate in my career to have worked with David Bowie, Ozzy Osbourne, Bono [from U2] and Eddie Vedder [from Pearl Jam], Robert Plant – I've seen a few singers that's for sure – and Tarja is very impressive.

"I was aware of Tarja before I had the opportunity to work with her. Back in 2006, I was in Finnvox Studios in Helsinki, recording *Venus Doom* with the Finnish band HIM, and Nightwish happened to be in another room. [They were mixing *Dark Passion Play* at the time, their first album without Tarja.] I'd sat and talked to the guys in the band, so I was aware of Tarja and who she was. The first opportunity I'd had to work with her was on a song called 'Until My Last Breath'. I had just moved from Los Angeles to Texas and it was the very first song that I mixed in my new studio. It was very challenging for me because I wanted Tarja to be happy with the mix, but at the same time I was worried because I was in new surroundings. Still, it all went very well, she was very happy, and we've been working together ever since.

"During this modern age of recording, it's rare that an artist will come along and be part of the mixing process. One of my favourite things about working with Tarja is that she does just that. She and her husband Marcelo will send me the

music, I work it up to 90 per cent and then we finish it together. They will fly to Texas, stay nearby and be at the studio every day. I really appreciate the time that we get to spend together. We see things very similarly and it's just great to be able to close the mixes knowing that the artist has approved everything on the recording. Marcelo has a very clear vision of how he ultimately sees the record, and between them, it's very easy for me to understand the direction of the music and how it should be. I think that's why we work so well together.

"I remember when Tarja's daughter Naomi was born, she brought her along to the studio when we were mixing *Colours in the Dark*. It was a challenge for her to look after such a young child, so my two daughters played with Naomi while we were

working. Our two families have become very close because of that and it's made the relationship extra-special.

"Tarja is unique among vocalists because she's a classically trained signer with a three-octave range, yet she's singing rock music. More importantly than that, Scandinavian [and Nordic] musicians have a very different sense of melody compared to American rock 'n' roll, which was based very much on the blues. Although the Finns embrace that too, their cultural roots come from the Vikings and the Norsemen, so their sense of melody is very different. There's a very strong classical side to Finnish music, and Tarja takes a lot of influence from there as well. Finland brought us bands like Hanoi Rocks, who influenced Guns N' Roses and changed music forever. It's a real hotbed of music.

"In my opinion, Tarja has never rested on her laurels and become static. She sees the importance of progression and change, and her music evolves all the time. We've made records that are very reverb-heavy and textural, yet more recently we've made records that are much drier and much more in-your-face. I think it keeps things fresh and leaves the audience wanting more. She manages to strike the perfect balance between singing classical and rock, and I think that's important, too, because a lot of people enjoy both sides of her voice. Nobody wants to get stuck in one genre, just as no one wants to live in one place or go to one restaurant. I think it's important not only for her as an artist, but also for the listener who gets something new each time, and I think we've succeeded in that."

BELOW Tim Palmer has become an important part of my sound over the years. I worked with him for the first time on my second album and when my daughter was still very small. Tim and his beautiful family made us feel very welcome and it was the start of a long-lasting friendship.

I saved my solo version of 'Medusa' and released it on the *Left in the Dark* companion album along with some of the demos, instrumentals and alternative mixes. I always enjoy hearing how other artists' songs have progressed during the production process and I wanted to share those moments with my die-hard fans.

◆◆――――◆◆――――◆◆

Costumes and makeup play a huge role when it comes to creating an image for performing, album artwork or a video. When I was in my late teens I wore some terrible clothes. I started dyeing my hair black and wore head scarves with long hippy skirts. I was still a student when I started singing in Nightwish and was not interested in fashion at all. I would never wear some of the clothes I wore at the beginning now, and I cringe when I see those photos. There was nobody to help or direct me with my style back then.

Sirja has been creating my outfits since around 1998, when I was still in Nightwish. We had lost contact when I went to high school in Savonlinna, but when Nightwish began, she saw an article about me and made contact through the band's website. I called her immediately and we met that same night. It was like we had never been apart. She is beautiful and I wanted her to become my dressmaker from then on. It is so nice to work with your friends because it is so easy to design things as a team, to get inspired by something and brainstorm together. We exchange ideas for new designs all the time. I look at high-fashion images online and send her pictures, then she comes back and asks me for more details. I give her the colours and she goes to the shops to find materials, then she sends me different pictures of what she has found. I trust her because she knows my body shape and what I will and will not wear. We always link the outfits to the music of the album and the character I am portraying. She made the dress I wear on the cover of *Henkäys Ikuisuudesta,* which I wanted to be as red as it gets. It needed to be comfortable because I wanted to keep the dress to perform in and knew it should be a full gown. I was very happy that I was still able to wear it for the concerts marking the 10th anniversary of the album's release. Sirja also made the cloak I wear on the cover of *My Winter Storm* from some fabric I had bought in Thailand while I was on vacation with my husband.

TOP Sirja hard at work.

ABOVE I loved flying in the air as a phoenix. I truly miss these kind of demanding sessions that take a lot of preparation. I really like the orange hair – do you think I should try that look on a permanent basis?

OVERLEAF I am where I am supposed to be, in front of the orchestra, during dark Christmas concerts in the Czech Republic.

IT IS SO NICE
TO WORK WITH
YOUR FRIENDS

I WANT TO
APPEAR AS A
POWERFUL
WOMAN

Another favourite designer of mine is Julia Trompert from Nordenfeldt, a German clothing company. Many years ago she contacted me about her brand and I really love her designs; they are very sophisticated but also very rock 'n' roll, feminine and strong. She made me the outfits for *In the Raw*, *The Shadow Self* and the hooded leather coat I wear on the *Colours in the Dark* cover. Some of the clothes I wore on the TV show, *The Voice of Finland*, were hers, too. I have a full wardrobe of her designs and have been wearing them for promotions, tours and more. Sirja and Julia are both very important when it comes to my image.

Just as I do not like to repeat myself musically, I like every album cover to look different but to still carry the hallmarks of my style. Most of the clothing I wear on the albums' artwork is also used in my shows, so each garment has to be very comfortable – they might not look it, but they are. Usually the fabrics are breathable, but not always. I wear a lot of fake leather material and things that have some shine so they look good under the lights.

Wearing synthetic fibres is more important to me than ever. My daughter is the first to ask, "Is that real leather? Is that from an animal?" I would never wear fur, not even for a photo session. I have a super-beautiful fake-fur jacket that I like to wear on cold winter nights. Most of my stage clothes are slightly altered from the album art to make space for the microphone monitor or have some stretch material added at the sides so I can breathe more easily. The materials that I use, even for the album covers, are super-stretchy. We make lots of clothes for the cover shoots but not everything ends up in the photos so we have lots of unseen items ready to wear on stage. They are extravagant and putting them on gives me strength. They are like theatrical costumes and they change my personality when I put them on. I want to appear as a powerful woman, but I do not want to reveal too much. I never want to appear as a sex symbol but as a strong, feminine, powerful woman and so the clothes need to convey that and have impact.

The outfit I wore on the artwork for *The Shadow Self* and *The Brightest Void* was very shiny and I was also wearing a lot of feathers at the time. I even wore feathered eyelashes because they were very fashionable. My tastes have changed a lot over the years, though, and now I take a lot of inspiration from what is going on in the world of high fashion. I really love Rick Owen and Alexander McQueen – they create some amazing designs. I love wearing colours but my clothes are mainly black as I feel that it

suits me best. It goes with everything and works for every occasion.
I have even worn it at summer weddings and while singing in church at
my friends' weddings.

When I was starting out with Nightwish, the gothic fashion scene was very
popular, but it was completely new to me. Some of my outfits from that
period were influenced by it but I didn't want to go too gothic because I
was not familiar with the style. Even now, I am labelled "the gothic queen"
and I do enjoy the drama of that look although I do not take much
stylistic inspiration from it.

Metallic finishes, especially gold, were nice discoveries. I had never
worn gold in my life, but on the cover of *In the Raw* it looked so strong
under the stage lighting. I was cursing myself for not trying it sooner.
My mother always wore gold earrings and I can see myself wearing
them too, when I am 60 or 70 years old.

For my classical appearances, you will usually see me wearing dresses
because I don't need to move too much. Those outfits need to be
comfortable enough for me to breathe properly, but are generally
more classy and elegant than my rock outfits. Because my classical
performances take place in churches or theatres, some audience
members come wearing suits and are really dressed up.

Heeled shoes and boots are also really important because I am smaller
than people think. When they meet me in the street, they often remark,
"You're so small!" Even my doctor says to me, "Where on earth does that
voice come from?"

My makeup artist Heidi Reponen has worked with me for as long as Sirja.
She was there when we released *Wishmaster* (2000). I met her when she did
my makeup for a magazine shoot and she was really good, talented and
funny. I enjoyed working with her and she has been there for me ever since.
She knows my face like no one else. She always makes me look so beautiful
and I dream of being able to do my own makeup as well as she does. As
with Sirja, I give Heidi some direction. I tell her which colours I want her
to use and what my outfits will be like and she prepares everything. She
always comes with an arsenal of makeup to add to my own, and from that
she creates my look and it's always a surprise. We don't always have the
chance to practise the looks beforehand, but when she did the makeup for
My Winter Storm, we had a dress rehearsal for the Ice Queen and The Doll.
The Ice Queen had a weird shape for the eyes, so that was a one-off. We
also practised *The Shadow Self* makeup, too. Heidi has done the makeup
for all my big releases and she has created some crazy looks.

TOP I have to admit I have a fetish
for high heels, but these have caused
me big problems, so I have to find a
solution fast before I do my next shows.

ABOVE My friend and makeup artist
since 1998, Heidi Reponen has always
made me look beautiful, except maybe
on this occasion when we were creating
the Dead Boy character for the 'I Walk
Alone' video.

RIGHT I have admired the view from the Rock of Gibraltar before – but never in 10cm high heels which gave me vertigo when I came close to the edge. Unfortunately, you can't see the shoes here.

BELOW The filming of the 'No Bitter End' video was the first band performance session I did with my musicians. The heat inside the venue was intense and we were sweating like we would in a normal show.

I have worked with a few other makeup artists: Maia Rohrer from Argentina did the *Act I* promotional photographs, and I used Laura Rantaniemi, who I met at *The Voice of Finland*, for the video shoots of 'No Bitter End' and 'Ave Maria'. Mari Vaalasranta, who I also worked with at *The Voice*, came with me to Florence and Milan in Italy for *Act II*. But Heidi is the main makeup artist in my life and she has given me lots of tips and products. Having said that, if I have to do shows I mostly do my own makeup.

My eyes have always been important to my image, and I have always been very careful that whoever is doing my makeup emphasises them. They are the windows to the soul – and for the record, I have green eyes. I know there has been a lot of discussion about this! I would never wear different-coloured contact lenses because I love their natural colour – my mother had green eyes, too. Although I use semi-permanent makeup on my eyebrows, I would never have cosmetic surgery. I don't like my wrinkles, but who does? I like to leave things as they are and like to think that my way of singing is a bit like facial yoga because it stretches the facial muscles and even neck muscles, too. I love exercising and doing sports, using the pool and running. Staying fit, healthy and slim is important to my image.

I am very particular about the products I use on my skin. I like natural, cruelty-free brands that can withstand the strong lights. I sweat a lot onstage and do not want my skin to absorb any nasty chemicals. I use skincare products recommended by a cosmetologist and make sure I cleanse my skin every morning and evening. I always remove my makeup before I go to bed and smother my skin in cream. I need a lot of moisture, especially when I go back to northern countries where the climate is drier. I take a little cosmetic bag with me for flights and apply hand cream and moisturiser over my makeup.

ABOVE These photos were taken during filming for *The Voice of Finland*, but these talented women have done my makeup on several occasions, including for video shoots and press events in Finland and abroad.

You might not know this, but I am a natural blonde and have been dyeing my hair black since I was a teenager. Again, I like to use products that are cruelty-free and as natural as possible. I have lost a lot of hair through using extensions over the years, but I swear by Maria Nila's vegan haircare range. Her shampoos and treatments work so well for me. My own hair is very fine, so I use wig pieces onstage and in photos to get the volume right.

It always takes a long time to plan and execute the visual look of an album and my style in combination with it. I had a real blast working with the golden theme of *In The Raw*, but while doing that I was already thinking about the next one to come: the platinum look for my *Best Of* album and, as you have already seen, the cover of my book.

8

WORTH
a thousand
WORDS

I am a positive person and I realise that fans who buy my records, follow my concerts and come to my 'meet & greets' feel that there is something special about my music. Without this "storm" of mine, I would not be here doing what I do, and it is a privilege to be able to earn a living from working as an artist. I am very dedicated to my music and my art: it is my life, my way of being. My story speaks to people, some of whom might see me as a phoenix who has risen from the ashes and fought her way to where she is now. Perhaps younger women see me as empowering, as someone strong to follow, and I feel a responsibility towards them and am very careful about how I appear. I know I have a lot of young followers who might be struggling with life, and that they find some comfort in my music is such a boost for me. It gives me the strength to continue.

I work extremely hard and always search for the positives in life; I will only work on projects that I feel very passionate about. When I was 15 or 16 years old, I remember my mother telling me, "You must not build castles in the sky: you need to be real and stay real for your own sake. There is no way you can think you're better than somebody – you do your thing." I can still hear her voice and she would have beaten the heck out of me if she thought I was trying to become something I am not! I have always kept my feet on the ground and stayed true to myself.

So many people tell me that they have found encouragement through my music because I often talk about my dreams, so I feel as though I am helping my fans to be strong. It is really important to me that this message of strength and positivity is conveyed through the artwork that appears on all my albums, singles and promotional images. I want to paint pictures and tell stories through these photos and I am very lucky to have worked with so many wonderful photographers over the years who have understood my vision. I have always had the freedom to be who I am and express myself in the way I choose. Even as my image has changed, I have never had someone standing behind me saying, "Why don't you go in another direction?"

When I originally recorded *My Winter Storm*, the record label had wanted to put my face on the cover, but I was not yet ready for that kind of attention. I am not a pop star and did not feel comfortable being portrayed as one, so we reached a compromise with Jens Boldt photographing me in character as the Ice Queen. Jens is super-talented, and I really wanted to work with him – he has shot so many famous artists, including Muse, Iggy Pop and Rammstein, who I was listening to a lot at that time. He created the winter scenes you see on the cover in his studio in Berlin and the results are incredible. The shoot took two days but he really captured my soul. There was another Rammstein connection with the packaging, as I wanted to involve Dirk Rudolph on the design. He had been behind some of their great artworks and also that of Finnish band Apocalyptica, so I knew he would be perfect for this. He was a great person to work with as he prefers, as do I, to create an artwork based on a real photo as opposed to a computer-generated design. The white dress I am wearing in the photos inspired the photographer to create the tree-like snowy scenery. It was like a movie: we had real branches in the studio and a beautiful Siberian husky dog which we used on the cover of 'The Seer' EP. I felt that when you looked into that animal's eyes you could see another world. The snow was fake, though, and there was so much of it that it got everywhere. It was in my nose and eyes, I was crying and couldn't breathe – but it looked so real. That was such a huge production and we shot all four characters from the album – it was less *The Chronicles of Narnia* and more *The Chronicles of Tarja*! For the Phoenix, I had to climb a high ladder and hang suspended around 10 metres up in the air so the material of my dress would fly around me. It was a lot of work with very long days, but it was beautiful, and my friend, makeup artist Heidi Reponen, had the time of her life creating all the looks. There was so much creative input from so many people. I loved it. And then came the video that accompanied the first single, 'I Walk Alone'.

ABOVE We had a great time with photographer Jens Boldt working on the photos for the artwork for my first and second albums. We created really inspiring images which have been praised by my fans.

OPPOSITE The ice queen was getting trapped with the forest attacking her. Having that crown of branches on my head was quite uncomfortable, but I was happy to put up with that to make the photos look gorgeous.

BELOW I loved The Doll character I created for the *My Winter Storm* album. Sometimes I would like to spend a little while watching the world go by through The Doll's eyes.

66

My story speaks to people, some of whom might see me as a phoenix who has risen from the ashes.

ABOVE This was the start of the second day of filming the 'I Walk Alone' video in Teufelssee, Berlin. Can't you just see the excitement on my face? I was dead tired, because I had only had a few hours' sleep after the intense shoot the day before.

LEFT It also happened to be my birthday on the day we filmed the video, and the crew surprised me with some gorgeous flowers.

For this clip, I used the director Jörn Heitmann, who I knew from shooting the video for Nightwish's 'Sleeping Sun'. I told him about the four characters that I wanted to feature in the storyline, and he came up with a *Hansel and Gretel* idea of two children meeting my different personas. Even at this early stage of my solo career, I knew I wanted all the videos to be connected to the album artwork so they would make a bigger impact. We shot it in the Grunewald Forest in Berlin, which is a beautiful area near Teufelsberg (German for Devil's Mountain). It was a tough session because we were battling the fading daylight and had to be sure all my makeup was ready in time so we could finish before it got too dark.

I had felt very comfortable and confident working with Jens and Dirk on the artwork so I used them once again for *What Lies Beneath*. I love working on the artwork for all my releases. I am quite old-fashioned in this, but I love putting in the time, sweat and effort. It gives things a deeper meaning for me. I remember the first time I saw the cover of *Eve* by The Alan Parsons Project, which was created by the famous design team Hipgnosis, who were also behind most of Pink Floyd's album covers. The *Eve* cover features two beautiful women who have huge warts, scars and blotches on their faces which you do not really notice at first. Only if you look closer can you see them. Inspired by that, I wanted my face to be on the cover of *What Lies Beneath*, but not as a standard beauty shot – I wanted to make people look twice. That was shot in my home studio in Finland when it was very cold. We used special-effects makeup to create the scars and moles that you see in the photos. Although some people naturally have these characteristics, I found it really spooky

ABOVE With director Jörn Heitmann after filming the 'I Walk Alone' video.

BELOW The creepy makeup effects for the cover art of *What Lies Beneath*.

to see myself looking like that. I work in an industry where a lot of women feel pressured into looking a certain way and showing off more than they would like to, and I feel it is such a pity that this kind of discrimination still exists – these photos challenge that. There is a similar pressure in the world of classical singing: when the Russian soprano Anna Netrebko began to emerge as a force in classical music, her face appeared on magazine covers, but instead of focusing on her beautiful voice, the media zoomed in on her sex appeal. There seems to be an inverse pressure in opera, where there is this cliché that you need to have a fuller figure to be an amazing singer!

ABOVE/ABOVE RIGHT Can you see me sleeping in the snow? Our neighbour was so kind to lend us the tractor that helped us get the perfect photos. Jens Boldt was checking if I was still breathing, but I was so cold I could barely feel my heart beating!

RIGHT I am still smiling in this photo. A moment later I jumped into the pool and the fabric of my dress started dragging me down and tangling around my legs – for a moment I really started to panic.

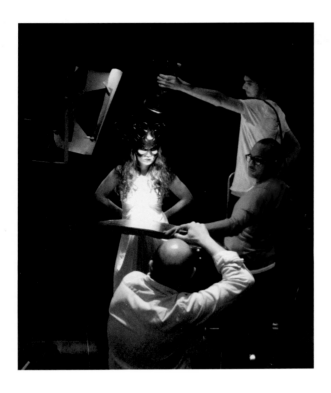

The first single from *What Lies Beneath* was 'Falling Awake' and I wanted the video to be a 'making of' from the recording sessions. It was done with my friends from Finland, Same-eYes, and I really enjoyed hanging out with friends, both musicians and film crew.

As we had the disagreement with Universal about the second single, with Germany wanting to release 'I Feel Immortal', while I wanted to release 'Until My Last Breath', I ended up going to Iceland to shoot videos for both with Jörn. I would never dare to freedive, but we found some astonishing footage of a diver that we thought would be great to use in the promo clip of 'Until My Last Breath' – there has never been a more appropriate title. I also shot another video for the UK release of 'Until My Last Breath' in Finland with Same-eYes, so we ended up having two videos for the same song.

ABOVE I was glad to have the same crew working with me on the artwork shoot for *What Lies Beneath* as I had for my first album. We used my vocal recording studio for all the indoor photos.

RIGHT I am blessed to have very talented friends in Finland. Same-eYes Production worked on the video for 'Until My Last Breath', which was filmed in a local Irish pub in Kouvola, Finland.

LEFT/BELOW Filming the 'I Feel Immortal' music video in Iceland was definitely the most exciting video I've shot so far in my career. I enjoyed every moment of being surrounded by its majestic landscapes. I can't wait to get back there to explore more of its beauty.

The story of 'I Feel Immortal' is reflected in the video with the whole circle-of-life narrative, it was very emotional, and shows how you must live your life to the fullest. I agreed on the video story with Jörn and we went with it. I had always wanted to go to Iceland but had never been until the proposal came to shoot there for four days. It was pretty cold, as you'd expect, but the scenery was so beautiful, with absolutely gorgeous waterfalls and rock formations. There were no trees, the beaches are black and I was walking around in the cold water with my dresses getting soaking wet. It was so amazing to be there, though. Some people have likened aspects of this video to Madonna's 'Frozen', and I have always loved that song so perhaps there was some subliminal inspiration. At the beginning of my solo career, I tried to record a version of 'Frozen' but my range is very different to Madonna's and it did not work out at all.

In order to get the perfect cover for *Colours in the Dark*, I travelled all the way to India. Colour was on my mind when I came across some very striking pictures on the internet. I soon realised they had all been taken by the same photographer, Poras Chaudhary, and decided that I would really like to work with him. Many of his photos were taken during the Indian Holi festival, which is also known as the festival of colours because coloured powders are thrown around and people smear them on their faces. Although I have yet to experience the Holi festivities in person, seeing these beautiful images really inspired me and it was only afterwards that Holi celebrations started popping up around Europe (and my idea became quite fashionable).

Poras was super-excited to work with me and it was my first time in India. He lived in a little town three hours from New Delhi, so Marcelo and I travelled there and it was like nowhere I had ever been before. It was a very poor town and there was a lot of sadness around but there was colour everywhere: on the walls, on people's clothing. We saw people who had absolutely nothing and, at one point, I remember a woman coming up to us at the traffic lights to offer me her baby girl. "Give her a good life," she told me. I was only a few months' pregnant but it really shocked me that a mother could be so desperate that she would give up her child like that.

ABOVE The moment before I entered the beautiful world of colours.

"I wanted to show the colours of life in those pictures

ABOVE It felt really strange to be standing in the middle of this group of Indian men. They barely dared to look at me during the photo session for *Colours in the Dark*, but the results were incredible.

RIGHT With photographer Poras Chaudhary.

Dirk Rudolph,
graphic designer

"*My Winter Storm* was my first Tarja project. The team already had the ideas and a photographer, so I was brought onboard to redesign the Tarja logo and come up with the rest of the packaging. I already knew a little bit about Tarja and my first impression was of how focused she was. She and Marcelo are their own creative directors. They know exactly what they want, and you don't often find that among musical artists.

"I wanted to base Tarja's logo on the pronunciation of her name: it has a strong consonant at the beginning and then it flows like an explosion. There are lots of dots and lines that make up the logo and you'll notice a few minor changes here and there across the different artworks, but the logo has mostly stayed the same over the years. The one exception was *Ave Maria – En Plein Air*. I wanted that to be different from the rock albums and the original idea was to make the logo look like a church organ, but it was transformed to more of an Art Deco-style design inspired by the church's steeple.

"*What Lies Beneath* is my favourite cover. I love the idea behind it – one of flawed beauty. Tarja and Marcelo already had the photos, so my role was working out how to integrate the logo and other graphic elements. It was very time-consuming to add all the dots and the lines that flow across the design and my colleague, Pablo Lütkenhaus, got a very bad arm from doing it. At that time we worked with a mouse, rather than a stylus, so it was quite a painful process. As we were using different photos for each media format, I felt we needed to create an overall logo that was iconographic. We wanted to retain that idea of movement within the graphic design: those dots and lines look like symbols and they allowed us to move from the front cover to the back and the booklet, and to play around with the design.

"The idea for *The Shadow Self* and *The Brightest Void* was developed with Marcelo. One of the original ideas was to have Tarja going down a staircase that was created from her shadow. Another was to have her emerging from her shadow, which would be like a doorway on the wall. We were all really inspired by the title and Marcelo came up with the idea of the frames. I wanted to make it like a living picture – as though you're watching a moving portrait at an exhibition – so I created the 3-D frames digitally and added them to the photos."

ABOVE I met Dirk Rudolph for the first time during the video shoot for 'I Walk Alone'. He came to see me in Berlin and it was great getting to know him on a personal level. He has been a very important part of my artwork designs ever since the beginning of my solo career.

That photo session was nothing like the beauty shots I was used to doing for magazines or other albums. I wore no makeup, only the coloured powders on my skin. It was messy but fantastic. I wanted to show the colours of life in those pictures, and particularly how colourful my own life had been. The photos on the album and single artwork were not edited with Photoshop or similar programs: that is exactly how the scene looked. The light and the moment had to be perfect. Five guys threw coloured powder at me, and we had two seconds to take the shot and then move on to the next one. Not many photos were taken but it was a really good session. I wanted to work with Dirk Rudolph again, to design the artwork, because I loved what we had achieved in the past. He came up with the idea of creating a meltdown of colours spreading across the pictures and under the cover lines, logo and album title on the album cover. This gave a modern touch that contrasted with the photos which exuded more of a 70s vibe and reminded me of the Psychedelic rock movement.

To date, all of my album covers and artworks give a sense of what I hope you will experience when listening to the music. I am fascinated by how an album can become associated with a particular colour in my brain. And how each time I come across that colour, I like to listen to that particular album. The opposite is also true. Music, colours and senses are all inter-connected for me and I have always wanted to offer my fans much more than just music.

Ever since my first Christmas album, I have used alternate images on different formats and editions, which I really enjoy doing because I get to work with so many talented and inspiring people. We used variations of the cover image on the vinyl and special edition of *Colours in the Dark*, just as I continue to do with all my releases. The idea for this came largely from the sleeve of The Police's

Synchronicity. I love that album but didn't know that there were different versions of the sleeve art until many years later when I found another edition with different photos in the montage. I thought it was really interesting and I always like artists who are not afraid to go further with the material they have to hand.

For '500 Letters', a song about an obsessed fan, I shot the video with Florian Kaltenbach, who has worked on several of my videos. He came to Buenos Aires and we filmed it in an area called Tigre on the Paraná Delta. Tigre has lots of islands and the only way to reach them is to travel by boat – it is very similar to Finland where the Finns have their summer cottages in the archipelagos. The song and video explore a different perspective on obsession but we wanted to tease an aspect of it. You might notice I look very different in it than in earlier videos: I was not fully made-up and look more natural. I was not afraid of showing myself in this light. I wanted people to see that behind the music and my voice, I am just a normal person.

Florian also shot the video for 'Victim of Ritual', and it sees me spreading the colours for those victims of rituals that do not feel alive any more. It reflected the song so well.

For the companion album, *Left in the Dark*, I wanted to involve my fans in the artwork. We sent out a bunch of photos that we took with Poras in India in front of a white canvas; they were like silhouettes and people could do whatever they wanted with them. I received hundreds and hundreds of submissions and I really enjoyed going through them all. I have such talented and devoted fans and I think of *Left in the Dark* as a special album that I created together with them.

Although he has not been involved in any of my album artworks, Paul Harries is another photographer I really enjoy working with. He has taken a lot of my promotional photos and I am sure we will continue to work together. I have met some of the photographers I have used for my albums when doing interviews and photo sessions where I felt comfortable and inspired by them. It's nice to work with such talents. I love photography and I like that the photos in my album artworks tell stories, that they have something to say.

ABOVE We shot the '500 Letters' video with Florian on one of the islands in the Paraná Delta in Buenos Aires. I have never been good at rowing; I prefer boats with a motor, but we had great fun making a spooky video for my third album. It's a wonderful place to visit – I highly recommend it.

Ave Maria features another of my favourite artworks. We worked on the photo shoot with Eugenio Mazzinghi, who had taken the photos for *Act I, The Shadow Self / The Brightest Void* and for a shoot for *Rolling Stone* magazine, which was where we actually first met. Unfortunately, we were unable to shoot in the church in Finland where the album was recorded, so we took these pictures at Mazzinghi's studio in Argentina. Marcelo and Mika Koivusalo had taken some photos of the interior of the church and the magnificent organ while we were there and we used some of those in the CD booklet. I didn't want the artwork to look like a generic classical album as I am more of a rock soprano than a classical artist, so the image we selected has a lot of shadowing on it. We used a projector to reflect images from the inside of the church onto me – the organ, the keys, the window frames and seats – and once again Dirk Rudolph designed the cover, which I think is really beautiful.

ABOVE/LEFT Shooting the artwork for *Ave Maria – en Plein Air* with Eugenio Mazzinghi. The artwork for the album definitely doesn't look like that of a regular classical music album, even though, music-wise, that's what it is.

THIS PAGE For *The Brightest Void* album cover, we cast my shadow onto the wall and then cut my shadow out, so that for *The Shadow Self* artwork, I literally came through the shadow on the wall – symbolically representing the journey of self-discovery the album represents.

The themes I explored on the monochrome artwork for *The Shadow Self* and *The Brightest Void* could not have been more different. The albums are connected to each other and so the album artworks belong together. The idea for the set was developed in Argentina with my photographer Eugenio Mazzinghi. The way I am lit on *The Brightest Void* cover casts the shadow for *The Shadow Self*. It was created as a real life 3-D image because the album is about self-discovery and I wanted to show myself emerging from my own shadow, which we cut out of this really thick carbon material. To create the poses, I stood in front of a really bright, white light, while Eugenio made sure I was perfectly aligned with my carbon shadow. It was not easy and took a long time to get right but I really love the results. Once the images were taken, Dirk Rudolph completed the design with the photo frames and typography.

ABOVE Martin Müller is the video director I choose for my biggest live releases.

RIGHT This was where the movie *Corazón Muerto* and my video for the song 'An Empty Dream' were filmed – in a derelict, abandoned old building in the middle of Buenos Aires. My outfit is by Julia Trompert from Nordenfeldt.

LEFT/OPPOSITE There is an important message about domestic violence in the video of 'Innocence'. We shot the video with film director Mariano Cattaneo in Buenos Aires and my local musician friends and Alex appeared as the band.

The video for 'No Bitter End' on *The Brightest Void* was the first time I had made a full band performance video in my solo career. I had been working with the musicians for such a long time and wanted to involve them in a video and, as the song is energetic, it felt like the right time to do it. It was filmed by Martin Müller, who also shot *Act I* and *II,* and I like that it is so different. It's such a happy rock song that it would have made no sense for it to be any darker.

'An Empty Dream' was originally written for a horror movie called *Corazón Muerto* (2015). I was asked by the Argentinian movie director Mariano Cattaneo to co-write the song with him and Miguel Ricardo Borzi, and naturally when the time came to create a video for the song, I asked if we could work together. Some of the main actors from the movie also took part in the video, which was shot at the film location. We didn't have a huge production budget but it was great to work on a movie set. We worked with Mariano again on the 'Innocence' video which, as with most of my videos, I wanted to have a deeper meaning and to move people emotionally – I wanted it to be more like a short movie. The clip explores domestic violence and uses a technique I borrowed from Paul McCartney's video for the song 'Only Love Remains'. That was shot using just one camera in a single take with no cuts, and Mariano agreed to try it. It was very tough to shoot but it achieved the effect I wanted to have on the viewer—the one-camera aspect added a layer of intimacy that is unique. Walls were moved on the set, and I was running from the piano to the band in real time while the actors were playing their parts. All was set up for the climax in the very last shot of the video.

RIGHT I didn't lock the door!

BELOW It was amazing to play white-and-black characters in our photo session for *From Spirits and Ghosts*. We prepared all the materials needed in the studio in advance for these photos and I felt like I was in a scene from a movie.

Some people may have been surprised when they saw the cover of 2017's *From Spirits and Ghosts (Score for a Dark Christmas)* because it doesn't look very festive for a Christmas album! When I was a child, I used to love watching theatre actors putting on their makeup and wigs backstage and wanted to capture that on the artwork for this album. It is a very, very dark record and when thinking about the artwork I came up with the idea for two characters, Spirit and Ghost, who were inspired by my personal approach to Christmas. I didn't want to appear as myself on the cover and felt more comfortable hiding behind these characters. There is both darkness and light at Christmas; many of us have good and bad thoughts during this period and I wanted the artwork to reflect those two opposites. It is a time of the year when I feel, more than ever, surrounded by spirits and ghosts in the form of angels, or just memories of those who are no longer with us.

I asked the makeup women from Mijas Natural to find a completely white wig and a black one. My childhood friend Sirja created the Spirit and Ghost dresses for this album in just 48 hours. She sourced the material, flew into Spain from Finland with some basic design ideas and then sewed the gowns on my old sewing machine. They were huge and made from several metres of material but because we had to make them in a hurry, they still had pins in them when we shot the photos. She took them back to Finland afterwards so she could sew them properly for the concerts.

Photographer Tim Tronckoe came to Marbella, where we rented a storage unit and built the scene for the album cover and all the other photos. I bought hundreds of black and white candles for the shoot – some of which I still have in my home and have lit every Christmas since.

On the morning of the shoot I had a terrible migraine and did not know if I would be well enough to get through the day, but it went away with the excitement of the shoot. It was a long, long day because we shot both characters that same day – I needed a shower in between to wash off all the makeup! As I was already made up, we recorded the videos at the same time. We started very early in the morning and finished very late at night but it was worth it. It speaks of the freedom I have that my label was

ABOVE The 'girl power' makeup and hair team from Mijas Natural, Spain. It took a very long time to apply the makeup for the photos and the results were so real that my daughter was scared when she saw me.

willing to release a Christmas album that looked like that. These are among my favourite ever photos of me.

The finished cover artwork was created by Travis Smith, an American graphic artist who has worked with Opeth, Avenged Sevenfold and Devin Townsend, and – more relevant to me – he'd created the cover for my first Christmas album, *Henkäys Ikuisuudesta*. I adore his work and his Opeth covers in particular are very beautiful. He always creates dreamy and unusual-looking covers and I wanted him to lend his magic to Tim's already fantastic photos.

I also worked with Tim on *In the Raw*, which once again was a completely different concept. The cover images were to be majestic and I wanted to shoot them as close to the centre of the Earth as we could get. The whole concept revolved around the idea of gold as a pure element, raw in nature, but a symbol of sophistication at the same time, and how you can find gold deep in the earth which originally came from asteroids that impacted millions of years ago. I had visited a breathtaking limestone cave in Gibraltar called St Michael's Cave, which has been there since prehistoric times. As this location was as close to the centre of the earth as we could get, we arranged to use it for a photo shoot. We took some images outside the cave at dusk and then went inside and worked all through the night, when there were no tourists. The cave has many different chambers and is also occasionally used for concerts so we knew it was safe, but it was a very challenging session because there was no natural light coming from anywhere. The cave formations look magical contrasted with the gold dress I am wearing on the cover. It was one of the best photo sessions ever and I was so happy to find such an amazing location.

Although we did not use the cave in any of the videos for *In the Raw*, we had a lot of fun exploring some very different ideas. 'Railroads' is one of my favourites because it involves my fans. I received hundreds and hundreds of video submissions that made me laugh and cry. I felt so proud of my fans – their courage and their loyalty was humbling. Florian was to direct the

ABOVE St Michael's cave is a super-inspiring and demanding location for taking photos. I was just afraid of seeing spiders, even though everyone was telling me there wouldn't be any.

The whole concept revolved around the idea of **gold** as a pure element, raw in nature, but a symbol of **sophistication** at the same time

ABOVE I have had the pleasure to work with director Florian on three very different music videos and I'm sure there will be more in the future.

BELOW Killer crow.

video for 'Tears In Rain', which made me cry a lot for unexpected reasons. When we were discussing concepts there were a lot of cheesy ideas going around, but I wanted to do something more significant and that I had never done before. Florian came up with the idea of filming a roller derby, and although I had not skated since I was a child, I agreed to do it. I didn't want to look like an idiot on roller skates and I had a week to train before we began filming. As roller skates have four wheels in two pairs at the front and the back, the centre of balance on them is very different from rollerblades where the wheels are in line. I practised at home and, when I felt ready, went to a skate park near my home to try it out in a larger space. The concrete surface in the skate park was much smoother than I was used to, and I began skating faster and faster. That was when I realised that I didn't know how to slow down and brake, and fell so hard on my butt that I thought I had broken my coccyx. I was screaming in complete agony. This was just three days before filming was due to begin and I had to ring Marcelo to collect me because I could not walk. I went to a doctor who performed manual therapy on my back, but I was in so much pain that I couldn't sleep or even walk, and had to fly to London while in excruciating pain. My character in the video is called Black Leijona (lion), which was very appropriate considering the colour of the bruise that had formed on my butt!

The roller derby girls were careful with me, but I still needed to fall in the video, and when I did it felt like I was on fire. I was crying with pain and there was a medic nearby to give me paracetamol and ibuprofen so I could finish the session. The story was about empowering women and me fighting, rising above my pain level – I can tell you that is real pain you see in my face, it was not fake! I am so grateful to all the women who were skating with me that day, they were so cool, so amazing and so encouraging, but I would have loved to have done that video painfree. It took me several months to recover from the injury, but I had to continue performing. I

LEFT These chicks really kick some ass! We were all sweaty but happy after the video shoot. I could barely stand because of the pain I was in, but again, it was worth it.

BELOW Another very glamorous makeup session with my friend and makeup artist Heidi Reponen. It was so hot outside and we couldn't find any shade, so the car boot had to do. Heidi came from Finland to Spain just for the photo session for *In the Raw* and left straight afterwards.

remember being at the Masters of Rock festival and not being able to jump at all but still wearing high heels. All of my crew were laughing about it, saying, "Shall we give you a clap on your butt?!" I now know that I can still rock with a broken butt, but I have not worn those skates since then.

It's important to me that all my album covers are different. I like to connect the artworks to the songs and give everything a deeper meaning. Marcelo always plays a big role – we brainstorm and he helps me a lot. We both work really hard to create ideas that are original. He also has a creative role in the music – he's the 'MIC' you see credited on my albums and we have written some lyrics together. Our working relationship has intensified over time, which I think is quite an achievement for a couple that has been together for more than 20 years. He is my rock, my pillar and the greatest partner in crime I can think of.

9

SELF
discovery

Being in the shadows is sometimes better than being in the light, although I never dwell too long on the darker side of life. When I began work on *The Shadow Self*, I was super-happy; my career was progressing and I was very inspired by the team who were there to support, embrace and go forward with me. That was such a big motivation. I had also been working very hard with my singing coach in Buenos Aires and felt I was getting back to classical singing, which naturally supports my rock singing.

In 2015, my calendar was really busy. I was asked to be one of the star coaches on the fourth season of the TV talent show *The Voice of Finland*, which I did alongside Michael Monroe from Hanoi Rocks. The show was such a fantastic learning experience and I realised I could help other singers by appearing on it, which was an amazing discovery for me. In the past, I had taught some classically trained students, but on *The Voice of Finland* the singers came from all different backgrounds. Nevertheless, I still had the knowledge and experience to help them. I took part in two seasons and my singers won both of them, so that was extremely gratifying. To film it, I was rushing between tours and the TV studios with my family, changing continents from South America to Europe to Asia and back to Europe again. I would love to do another series of the show, and am keeping my fingers crossed!

Although this was a crazy period, I was starting to feel more relaxed and confident in my work. I found myself on a new path towards self-discovery and this inspired me to write about opposites: love and hate, shadows and light – the opposing sides of us and of everything.

ABOVE My very comfortable (I lie!) chair on *The Voice*. It is still a pure pleasure to sit on that chair, though.

While I was reading around the subject, I came across an interview with Annie Lennox, where she spoke about the shadow self: it is the darker, hidden side that gives artists the freedom to create. This was a turning point for me because I had already been thinking along these lines.

As I have grown older, I have got to know myself, especially after the birth of my child and becoming a mother, and Annie's words really hit me. I thought about why I acted in certain ways – what was driving me? Some people might act weirdly in certain situations and afterwards, you wonder why. That is the shadow self calling and it is in all of us. Although I do not necessarily show other people my darker side, it expresses itself in my art. I wanted to embrace that side and make it into something beautiful. I never planned for it to sound a certain way, but the songs started to take their own shape. I was listening to Ozzy Osbourne's *Scream* album a lot during this period, and several other guitar-based albums which I was telling Alex Scholpp to listen to by Disturbed, Alice In Chains, Avenged Sevenfold, and even Slipknot – their song 'Psychosocial' is a great track with a really tough vocal line. Alex and I ended up writing 'Calling from the Wild' together as a direct result of this.

ABOVE When Michael Monroe recorded his vocals for 'Your Heaven and Your Hell' in Finland, he also recorded a sax solo. We had great fun.

I am surrounded by so many talented people from different backgrounds and I did not yet have the guts to do all the songwriting alone, so this album features a lot of collaborations with other artists and musicians. I have some very different songs and I wanted to match the musician to the style of each. To have that amount of freedom as a solo artist is fantastic.

Arch Enemy's Alissa White-Gluz became involved because of the idea of contrasts. I was recording my vocals for 'Demons in You' and I thought it would be really good to call her in because her voice is the opposite of mine, and a perfect match for this album and for the song.

During the filming of *The Voice of Finland*, Michael Monroe and I got very close, so I asked if he would like to do a song with me because I had a track that did not yet have any lyrics or melody. He jumped at it and later said that 'Your Heaven and Your Hell' was the heaviest and longest track he had ever co-written and recorded. He took it as a challenge. The following day, he came running to my dressing room with the lyrics. It was his idea to also play the sax and mouth organ on the song and we had a great time recording it. He is a genius, a living legend in Finland, and very talented with a great knowledge of music history. I did not want to miss the chance to work with him.

> # The show was such a fantastic learning experience

ABOVE With Miia Kosunen from my team, who won my first season on *The Voice of Finland*.

LEFT Suvi Åkerman from my team on my second season of *The Voice of Finland* celebrates her win.

BELOW My darling friend, *The Voice* coach colleague and songwriter Michael Monroe.

I had a lot of good material in hand for *The Shadow Self*, but there were too many songs for one album. I didn't want to make a double album because I felt that would be too long, but I also didn't want to waste the songs on B-sides. They were too good for that, so I came up with the idea of a prequel album, *The Brightest Void*, which represents the light that casts the shadow. Now I had two albums, I wanted to have some fun and include a few covers as well as some alternative versions. One of the most famous is 'Goldfinger', which was originally sung by Shirley Bassey for the James Bond movie of the same name.

Many years ago in Finland, I was invited to sing in a TV gala and cover some movie songs. 'Goldfinger' was one of these and I had a hard time with it, it is very demanding and my voice was not ready for it at the time. A few years later, I got an invitation to perform at a private party in Russia and decided to give it another go. I flew some of my Argentinian musicians over and we created a new arrangement of the song. This time I could sing it and decided to record it for *The Brightest Void*. I also decided to cover Paul McCartney's 'House of Wax', which is one of his darkest songs. He is a pop artist but on every one of his albums there is always a dark song and this one appealed to me. The darkness was calling and I just had to give it a try. I loved singing it.

My version of Muse's 'Supremacy' ended up on *The Shadow Self*. I remember the first time I heard the original, I thought: "What a great track, it would be amazing to have this with heavier guitars." I always felt they were missing from it. I have been a Muse fan since their 2009 album, *The Resistance*, and I even worked on one of the songs from that album with two of my singers on *The Voice of Finland*. Matt Bellamy is a fantastic singer, but our voices are very different. I screamed those high notes like crazy in the studio and as I did, the recording engineer and my husband were dying to laugh but they had to stay quiet during the recording. That song was a real toughie to record but the live performances are worse. Sometimes I hit the note and sometimes not. I love it, though, because it's fun and not a song that people would expect me to do.

My brothers Toni and Timo had already sung some backing vocals for my previous albums, but I always try to support Toni and kick his butt because he is very talented. I told him that I had this song, 'Eagle Eye', for him to sing which I thought would be perfect for his voice. It was also a celebration of our relationship as siblings and of making music together again. It is a very positive song that I wrote with Pauli Rantasalmi,

BELOW With my brothers Timo (left) and Toni. Thankfully, we are very close. I have been blessed to have such beautiful brothers who have supported me my whole life.

the guitarist from the Finnish rock band The Rasmus. The Rasmus have really catchy melodies which is exactly what I was looking for in this song. I was able to meet up with him in his studio because I was in Finland for such a long time with *The Voice of Finland*, and we sat down and wrote the song together based on a guitar riff he had. Toni and I recorded the song in my Finnish studio and it went on *The Shadow Self*. Every time I hear it I still get goosebumps when he sings.

Another track that gives me goosebumps on that album is 'Innocence'. It's really heavily inspired by classical piano and I knew I wanted to use piano in the middle-eight. I invited my old university friend Izumi Kawakatsu to improvise this section – she was in Noche Escandinava and is an amazing pianist. She prepared this beautiful improvisation that really captures the song and makes you sit up and take notice. Another musician I returned to was Mike Terrana, while others were new collaborations, including my drummer friend Fernando Scarcella from the Argentinean rock band Rata Blanca and Red Hot Chili Peppers' drummer Chad Smith. Chad came on board for the album because of my bass player Kevin Chown. He and Chad are very good friends and play in a band together called Bombastic Meatbats. He recorded four tracks with us in the end,

BELOW While I was touring my Christmas concerts in Germany, my friend Izumi Kawakatsu came to record the piano for the song 'Innocence' – those fingers are gold!

ABOVE My brother Toni came to record vocals for the song 'Eagle Eye' – it was a fun session.

ABOVE Alex and Jetro working on the guitar recordings in Buenos Aires.

TOP Fernando Scarcela recording drums for *The Shadow Self* in El Pie Studios in Buenos Aires.

ABOVE This was my large, purpose-built room for recording vocals. Here I am recording *The Shadow Self* album vocals with Jetro.

LEFT I have still not met drummer Chad Smith in person, but I was so glad and honoured to have him playing on my album. Here, we are talking about the songs he was about to record for *The Shadow Self*.

including an alternative version of 'Eagle Eye' which I put on *The Brightest Void*. He was recording with Kevin in LA and I was on a Skype call with them overseeing the recordings. It was fantastic to watch him play and I gave him free rein to come up with a bit of funkiness at the beginning of 'Demons in You', as a humble homage to his own band, Red Hot Chili Peppers. It was such an honour to have him involved.

'Undertaker' saw me revisit my time at Hans Zimmer's Remote Control Productions. I wrote it with the Hollywood movie composer Atli Örvarsson, who has also worked on the *Pirates of the Caribbean* series and *Angels & Demons* (2009). I met him during the making of *My Winter Storm* and told him that I would really like to work with him some day. It didn't happen for that album, but I got in touch with him again when I was working on this one, and he sent me a track that had originally been composed for a car commercial. It had an exciting, driving melody, and he said to me, "I only have this idea but I don't think it could suit for a voice." I took the track as inspiration and completely smashed it. When I heard the first lines of melody, I realised it could be turned into a rock track. It sounds like it should be on a movie soundtrack with all the strings, and the middle-eight is very orchestrated. Atli was very happy when he heard it. When you put music in someone else's hands, you can make magic, which is why I have always liked writing with people from different backgrounds. When it works, it is really fantastic, and it was so nice for me to go back to the Remote Control Productions team.

I really relied on my gut instinct for *The Shadow Self*, which was the first record in my career that I have produced at a distance. It really helped that I had already been working with most of the musicians for several years and we knew each other's strengths so well. In a way, it's sad that we're not able to go back to recording as a full band in the studio because I loved working like that, but luckily I now have the technology that allows me to be in touch with musicians on the other side of the world. It means

ABOVE I was told that this ship in Antigua was used in some of the *Pirates of the Caribbean* movies, so it inspired us to write the song 'Diva'.

OPPOSITE TOP We filmed the 'Leaving You for Me' video with Martin Kesici in the archipelago of Finland. I just love the whole Viking vibe in it.

OPPOSITE BELOW Every good session leaves a reminder. A goat attacked me while we were filming the video, and this is what I was left with for several days afterwards. (And check out those beautiful Nokia phones we had back then!)

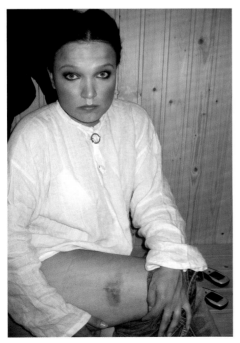

everyone can record at their own pace in their own studios and that's something that's made so many amazing collaborations possible.

I get requests from potential collaborators on an almost daily basis, but I don't have time to do everything and I have to feel that I can bring something to the project. Collaborations always teach you something and it is interesting to see how other artists work.

At the very beginning of my solo career, I sang with Martin Kesici on the single 'Leaving You For Me'. He was one of the winners of a German talent show called *Star Search* and the connection came through Universal Music in Germany. I loved his voice and the track was very beautiful, so I was glad to take on the challenge.

Jim Dooley, arranger

"I was introduced to Tarja through my work with Hans Zimmer. I didn't know who she was at the time because I was completely immersed in the film music business and not very familiar with contemporary pop music – but her idea to add Hollywood-style film scores to her music was groundbreaking. I'd never heard anyone combine a classical-style voice with rock 'n' roll the way she did. It's actually quite hard to do, and no one does it better than Tarja.

"For a star of her stature, I was surprised by how humble she was. Tarja is unique because she can write amazing melodies, beautiful lyrics, and perform at the highest level. She's also so kind and humble about it all. It's really mind-blowing. When we work together, it's all about the music and the creativity. Every time Tarja asks me to help her on a record she surprises me. I don't take our collaborations for granted. I'm honoured to have worked on each track on each album and I'm thrilled with how her most recently completed album, *In the Raw*, turned out and that I provided orchestral colours for her incredible writing. We respect and appreciate each other, which allows us to take risks and be bold. Over the years we've become great friends and I thoroughly enjoy when her family comes to stay with me in Los Angeles.

"'I Walk Alone' is my favourite Tarja song. It is one of the first songs I worked on with her and it will always hold a very special place in my heart. It's so bold and creative that I still get a rush when I hear it. I remember when I went to see her perform at the House of Blues in Los Angeles. That was the first time I saw her live. When she performed 'I Walk Alone', I was incredibly moved. Going backstage and sharing those moments after the show, knowing what we had created together, was electric."

ABOVE When I met Jim Dooley for the first time at Remote Control Productions, I remember how astonishing it was to see him "playing" the different orchestral instrument samples. I had never seen such a talent before, and I could only imagine him playing any instrument in the orchestra for real. I instantly connected with him and we have stayed friends ever since.

Schiller was an artist I had been a fan of for many years and he approached me to write the lyrics and melody for one of his tracks. 'Tired of Being Alone' came out in 2007 and was even nominated for a Grammy in the USA – my first and only nomination… so far.

Unfortunately, so many collaborations are done at a distance and we don't often get to work together in the same studio. For example, when I recorded 'The Good Die Young' – released in 2010 – with the Scorpions, I would have loved to have sung the song in the same studio as Klaus Meine, but sadly that didn't happen. That collaboration was such a surprise. I remember Marcelo and I were staying in our first home together in Buenos Aires when an email unexpectedly came through from the band's manager. I couldn't believe it. This was a super-important band from my youth: I had sung along to an incredible number of their songs and now they were contacting me to collaborate with them. How did they even know I existed? I later found out that the guitar player Rudolf Schenker had listed my first solo album as one of the best albums of 2007. Wow! They gave me two songs to choose from, but obviously neither was written for my voice so I struggled, but I did the best I could. We have since performed 'The Good Die Young' together live on a few occasions, and the last time we met was at Rock The Coast festival in Spain in 2019 where we were both performing separately. The drummer Mikkey Dee came to pick me up right after my show so I could go backstage with them. It was such a nice experience to see the guys again. I never would have expected to become part of their story.

Another unexpected collaboration was with Mike Oldfield. Torsten was working with Mike on his remix album and he asked if I would like to work on a song with them. The track had no lyrics or melody, so I was able to put my stamp on it. I sang on 'Never Too Far', which appeared on his 2013 remix album *Tubular Beats*. Mike is such a well-known artist and his *Tubular Bells* album was a big influence on so many people – I have always loved his sound and Marcelo has all of his albums in our record collection. Of course, he also collaborated with Maggie Reilly on 'Moonlight Shadow', which brought me in full circle back to one of my favourite childhood singers.

I have also loved collaborating with some of my contemporary female rock artists. During my youth, there were a lot of female rock artists whose music I followed and whose voices I adored, including Patti Smith, Bonnie Tyler, Ann Wilson from Heart and Kim Wilde. When I started out in my professional career, I didn't know many women who were doing the same thing as me. At the outset, the only metal band with a female singer that I knew of was Theatre of Tragedy and their then vocalist Liv Kristine. A little later, through playing festivals, I heard The Gathering and I got to meet their original vocalist Anneke van Giersbergen. But it was only really once I began my solo career that I connected with more female metal artists. I have gained a lot of support from them and vice versa, which has been wonderful.

Throughout my career, I have always been treated with respect and kindness. I have not personally experienced any sexism working in the metal industry but I understand that this is unusual. I have never been treated badly in that way and if I thought that was going to happen, I would cut that link short. Nowadays, there are even more female artists in metal, but I think the whole "female-fronted metal" genre is silly. Do we need to separate the sexes in this way? I still see myself as being part of a rock-metal movement and I am very happy and super-proud to be one of the women who rock.

When I was in Nightwish, I remember some journalists trying to suggest there was a kind of rivalry between me and the other female metal singers. I remember being asked about cat fights and if we were competing against each other. They were saying ridiculous things and I didn't know where it came from. What on earth would I have against these women? I feel that there is a sisterhood in metal, and I am proud to belong to it.

Doro was my first female collaborator and what an amazing woman she is to work with. She asked me to

BELOW She is wonderful and always very positive. I admire you, Doro Pesch.

TOP LEFT The beautiful Sharon den Adel. I have had such great chats and shared lovely moments with her. I love her to bits.

TOP RIGHT I met Floor Jansen and Liv Kristine at Doro's anniversary show in Germany some years ago. I have had the pleasure to sing with Liv and Floor on a few occasions in my career and it has always been amazing.

ABOVE It's so nice to bump into friends when you are working. Cristina Scabbia was performing with Lacuna Coil at the festival on the same day as me, so it was great to catch up with her.

LEFT Shooting 'The Paradise' video with Within Temptation in the Netherlands. What a great day!

sing on 'Walking with the Angels' on her 2009 album *Fear No Evil* and I asked if she would sing with me on 'The Seer'. She is a sweetheart and it has been so interesting to see how she handles her solo career. I was just taking baby steps at the time, but she has been doing this for a long, long time. I also got to perform with her at her big 25th-anniversary show in Germany. She is a remarkable person and someone I look up to.

The 2010s brought opportunities to collaborate with more of my sisters. It was always a matter of finding the time and now we have managed to do this. I first met Sharon den Adel from Within Temptation when I sang on their 'Paradise (What About Us?)' song that they released on their album *Hydra*, and I included a new mix of it on *The Brightest Void*. Although I recorded my vocals in Buenos Aires, we met up for the video and photo session and have performed the song together live many times, during their shows and mine. It is so lovely that one song has so much to give.

Cristina Scabbia from Lacuna Coil was someone I used to bump into a lot in hotel foyers and backstage at festivals. We would always hug and chat, but it was not until I recorded 'Goodbye Stranger' for *In the Raw* that we were able to sing together, although it had been in discussion for a long time. She is a very distinctive singer. Although I have not yet recorded with her, I finally met Amy Lee from Evanescence in 2019 when I was their special guest in Slovakia. She is such a sweetheart.

Of course, many of us don't just have our passion for music in common, but motherhood, too. To be a rock mum is to have a very rich life. I have talked with many women from the metal world about parenthood and it has been wonderful to share our experiences. When Simone Simons found out she was pregnant she wanted me to be the first to know, and I was so honoured. I have talked to Sharon den Adel and Floor Jansen about motherhood, too, and about how important it is to have an understanding partner – luckily, both of them have partners who work in the music industry.

Throughout the Covid-19 pandemic, I continued working with other artists. For instance, I collaborated with the power metal band Primal Fear for a special version of their rock ballad 'I Will Be Gone'. It's always a challenge when there are male and female voices together on the same track but it was a pleasure to do.

I have been really lucky to work with a lot of beautiful and different musicians in the past and of course there are many more I would love to collaborate with. My wish list is very long but Peter Gabriel, Sting or Roger Waters are definitely on my fantasy list.

BELOW Peter Gabriel has been a great inspiration for me. I was honoured to meet him backstage at his concert in Dublin while I was recording my own album nearby.

10
SPIRITS
and
GHOSTS

ABOVE This was the last Christmas we celebrated with our mum. Even though we were not having a traditional Christmas at home that year, we still did the thing I love the most about our Christmases – we found a piano and sang carols for hours together.

C hristmas has not been the same since my mother passed away. The bottom fell out of my world and my family had to find our own ways to celebrate. It took me years to process the situation and let her go. Christmas is meant to be a time when you are with your family and your loved ones, but unfortunately it is not always the case. I have heard stories about people who are alone for the holidays and count the days before they can go back to work and see other people again. For many, it is not an easy time. Music gives us comfort, hope and can embrace us during hard times, and I wanted to address this on my second festive album, *From Spirits and Ghosts (Score for a Dark Christmas)*.

Although I have a huge collection of Christmas albums, from jazz artists and Finnish classical singers through to Celine Dion and Cliff Richard, I do not have a favourite and perhaps this is why I decided to make my own. My first Christmas album, *Henkäys Ikuisuudesta*, was the album that I wanted and needed to make at that time. It had such a huge impact and even today my fans are still looking for that kind of music. It was a little darker and more melancholic than the more traditional releases and focused mainly on Finnish songs with a few international ones. For my second album, I deliberately chose songs that are better known all over the world so that it would resonate with a wider audience of those who had lost loved ones or who are just alone and lonely.

To find the right songs for my voice I went through trillions of records, both online and in my collection. I needed to find material that I was comfortable singing. I also wanted to do a German song because of my memories of living in Germany when I was studying at Karlsruhe. I loved the Christmas markets there and would get so excited when they started to appear. They sell many delicious foods and drinks, such as glühwein and gingerbread – all with very similar tastes and smells to Finland and so comforting when the air is a little chilly.

The song I chose to record was 'O Tannenbaum' (O Christmas Tree), which I remember hearing everywhere and is very traditional. We have a Finnish version called 'Oi Kuusipuu', too. My friend Torsten helped me record it and after we were done he congratulated me, saying that I had the accent of an old German native, which was very pleasing to hear.

As with the other album tracks, that song differs from the original version and the idea for that came from Jim Dooley. He has worked on all my orchestral arrangements since *My Winter Storm* so we've known each other for a long time now. A while before we started working on this album, he played me some Christmas tracks he had worked on and I thought they sounded great. They had weird orchestral arrangements and were very different from anything else I had heard. I discussed the possibility of doing a complete album with him – I had always wanted to do another Christmas album – and so when the time came, I asked him if he would like to join me. I gave him the directions and explained that the songs needed to be really dark. We tried out a couple and went back and forth with the ideas until he got it. I would say to him: "It needs to be this dark; from major chords to minor!" I remember hearing Annie Lennox's version of 'God Rest Ye Merry Gentlemen', and she had a very beautiful choir and vocal arrangement, but I wanted mine to be much darker. It was amazing that Jim understood my vision. He gave all the songs completely new lives, which is something I usually do with rock covers, changing the original into something of my own. Instead of those happy Christmas songs, we went more in the direction of *The Ring* (2002) score or *The Nightmare Before Christmas* (1993) – those movie soundtracks were a big inspiration and I was telling Jim, "Think of Danny Elfman (composer of *The Nightmare Before Christmas*) when you're scoring this." Other composers who influenced this album were James Horner, who made the soundtracks to *Titanic* (1997) and *Avatar* (2009); Harry Gregson-Williams' darker, weirder stuff, such as *Shrek* and *The Chronicles of Narnia*; and even Steve Jablonsky, who composed the soundtracks to *The Texas Chainsaw Massacre* and the 2010 reboot of *A Nightmare on Elm Street*. You can still recognise the songs, but they go in a completely different direction.

> I remember hearing Annie Lennox's version of 'God Rest Ye Merry Gentlemen', and she had a very beautiful choir and vocal arrangement, but I wanted mine to be **much darker.**

Take a song like 'Feliz Navidad': I hate the original. It is not one of my favourite Christmas songs and yet it is probably one of the most played, ever. We had to completely forget about the original in order to transform it.

As Christmas is associated with gifts and goodwill, I decided to re-record 'Feliz Navidad' to help raise money for an important cause that is close to my heart – Barbuda Relief and Recovery. Between August and September 2017, major hurricanes destroyed some of the Caribbean islands and Barbuda was one of the islands devastated by Hurricane Irma. All the residents had to flee their houses and it was devastating. I love the Caribbean so much and wanted to help them rebuild in some way, so I sent out an SOS to all my friends in the industry and they responded immediately. The single features so many amazing singers, including Michael Monroe, Cristina Scabbia, Tony Kakko, Floor Jansen, Doro Pesch, Elize Ryd, Marko Saaresto, Timo Kotipelto, Simone Simons, Joe Lynn Turner, Hansi Kürsch and Sharon den Adel. The recovery work is still ongoing, but I was happy to be able to help and my label, earMUSIC, offered to double the amount of money raised, which was just fantastic.

One of the most amazing things about this album is the instrumentation. It sounds like we had a full orchestra involved but actually everything you hear are samples – audio recordings of individual instruments which are blended together to create a full band or orchestra – and the results sound fantastic. Those samples still have all the colours, the nuances and the fragility of a full orchestra. When I was working on my first record, I learned that all the major Hollywood composers' soundtracks – the ones that sound so awesome – use samples to create a solid foundation for the full orchestral recording, with the soloist layered on top. They then mix everything together so that it has the feel of a real orchestra but with the perfect tempo of the samples. These guys have access to

ABOVE Recording another Christmas album during the summer! This time around, the location was Antigua, where the palm trees were swinging, and the air was very warm. Torsten was recording my vocals and it was a very relaxed session.

OPPOSITE One of the many Christmas concerts I have done in Finnish churches.

Tim Tronckoe, photographer

"Every photoshoot has its special moments so it's really impossible for me to pick an absolute favourite, but for *From Spirits And Ghosts* we were able to create our own set, and the pictures are just so wonderful. There's one photo where Tarja in the white outfit is having a conversation with Tarja in the black outfit. Obviously, we had to Photoshop it, but it just looked so cool. I love the results when she looks into the camera; she's so captivating, so mesmerising. I also fondly remember when we shot Tarja at Wacken Open Air. Alissa White-Gluz from Arch Enemy was performing but she arrived a day early so we could take some photos for the 'Demons In You' artwork. It was a brief session and I only had a tiny dressing room where I could set up, but those pictures are so great and they really show the friendship between the pair.

"A few years ago, Tarja took part in my *Portraits* book and I portrayed her as Anne Boleyn. We combined it with the *From Spirits And Ghosts* photoshoot and she was so completely into her role as the queen. The results were phenomenal. The dress worked so well and the setting was amazing: again, it shows how versatile Tarja is. Once you give her an idea, she takes it and makes it her own; she's so incredible when it comes to that.

"Working with Tarja has always been a lot of fun. Our first full session was in 2016 in a studio in Nuremberg, Germany, for *The Shadow Self*. I had a couple of ideas, she brought the outfits and we shot some very powerful pictures that were very strong and dramatic. It got a little more challenging after that because I was asked to go to Italy in November where Tarja was going to record her live DVD, *Act II*. She wanted to shoot some pictures in the streets of Florence and we decided to just go for it. Every year, there's a big marathon held in Florence and less than 24 hours before we were due to do our shoot, we found out that it was going to be on the same day. While Tarja was getting ready at the hotel, my assistant and I went to Piazza della Signoria in the city centre to come up with a plan. It's a beautiful area, with all these incredible sculptures – you can see Cellini's bronze statue Perseus with the Head of Medusa there – and it's part of the Museum of Florence. One of my friends can speak Italian and he got the museum staff to agree to allow us to use the entire piazza while the marathon was on, as no tourists were allowed there while it was taking place. We had the area to ourselves thanks to that marathon and we shot so many unbelievable pictures. I think those are some of my all-time favourite pictures of Tarja. It was cold and windy that day, and Tarja had a really bad cold, but she was so professional, she really pulled it out of the bag. Those pictures are amazing. They show how strong and beautiful Tarja is and they also capture the classical surroundings of the city.

"Another great photoshoot was in Gibraltar for *In the Raw*. It was in St Michael's Cave, which is hard to get to but worth it. It was a night shoot; we started at seven in the evening and we finished at maybe two or three in the morning. As it was getting darker and darker, it gave this beautiful, dramatic view of Spain and Morocco and that added even more to the pictures. The area outside the cave was full of monkeys and they tried to steal our gear when we weren't looking so we had to be super-careful. Once inside the cave, we were safe, because apparently the monkeys are claustrophobic and don't like it in there. Although the cave is open to tourists, it's very rough inside and it's tough to place your lights, to move around and to find a good

ABOVE This guy is just a thrill. Our photo sessions with Tim Tronckoe have all been very different, but always super-productive and inspiring. Tim is a great talent and over the years we have really got to know each other and become friends.

spot to show off the grandeur of the place. However, the results were just phenomenal and way beyond both our expectations.

"I still remember the first time I met Tarja. It was in 2016 and she was the headline act at Metal Female Voices, a festival in Belgium where I live. I had a little photo booth backstage where I had already shot a couple of the artists and I asked Marcelo if it would be OK for Tarja to stop by and have some photos taken before the show began. I was meant to have about five minutes with her, but that quickly became more because Tarja really loved the images I was taking and decided to get some more before her show. I'm a metal fan and she's

such an iconic artist, but I wanted to capture her in a different way. During that entire session she was just so lovely and kind, a real pleasure to work with. I couldn't have imagined where it would lead.

"Tarja has always been so welcoming and she really cares about me and about the end results. She appreciates what I do; my art, my craft. There's always so much drama in the pictures but there's never any actual drama during the photo sessions because she's so professional. She always gives so much; she's so passionate, so humble and down-to-earth. I'm very lucky to work with someone who is, both professionally and personally, such a sweetheart."

huge libraries of insanely beautiful samples, and I really wish I had access to everything they do on my computer.

As with my first Christmas album, we recorded my vocals over the summer, but this time we recorded in the Caribbean instead of Finland, and I did not put up any decorations. In the morning I would go for a swim in the sea, and then come back and record a song. At the end of the day, we would have a barbecue with Torsten and the next day, we would do the same thing. Some days we would lose the internet or electricity, or it would be raining cats and dogs and we would have to pause because the sound of the rain would come through on the recordings, but it was very relaxed, very peaceful and I needed to maintain that calm in my voice. I really enjoyed singing over the top of Jim's orchestral tracks. I could really imagine I was standing in front of the orchestra but at the same time it was a huge challenge because I had to control my voice. I could not use my full voice as I did for my *Ave Maria* album. I needed to be more fragile and not blow up the volume.

My daughter Naomi joined me on 'Deck the Halls'. She loves the song and when she was humming it, I said to her, "Would you like to sing with Mummy?" She was very small, only about five years old at the time, and it was a very spontaneous thing. We stood her on a chair with headphones on and she sang next to me. We did two takes and it was done. She is very proud of hearing her own voice and we got to perform the song together twice in Moscow in December 2018. I think I was more nervous than her, but it was a fantastic moment for both of us. I would love to sing again with her one day, but would never push her into it. I think learning the arts is good for children and she has a lot of talent for it.

Alongside all the traditional Christmas tunes, I wanted to have an original song on the album, too. My own festive track, 'Together', came about really quickly, and I broke all the rules on it. It doesn't have a repeating chorus, but just one chorus instead and it didn't need any more than that. It's about lonely people at Christmas who long to share their time with someone else. No one is meant to be alone and I believe that we are always meant to have someone in our lives.

ABOVE Once in a lifetime you must spend Christmas in New York, right? We wanted to experience that as a family, and now when Naomi sees the big Christmas tree in the movies, she always says how big it is in real life.

OPPOSITE The lineup of a Raskasta Joulua show in Finland.

This album also offered something different in the form of an accompanying graphic novel. It was the idea of the label, earMUSIC, and I loved it. We wanted to do something really special to go along with this strange-sounding Christmas album, so it was not a 'normal' graphic novel. I chose the artist Conor Boyle from a shortlist and he took inspiration from my song 'Together', which captures the whole concept of the album being about lonely people at Christmas, as well as my lyrics and the two characters I created for the album artwork. Peter Rogers wrote a wonderful story to accompany it and I was so pleased to see the finished book.

Once again, the album was mixed by Tim Palmer. I wanted to involve him because he has been part of my career for a long time and gives me very good feedback. He was so surprised by the album because nothing like this had been done before. In 2017, the year the album was released, I became a guest performer with Raskasta Joulua. Formed in 2004 by Erkka Korhonen, the project has a rotating lineup and involves performing heavy-metal versions of known Christmas songs in Finland. It is a lovely idea and so many famous singers have participated over the years. When I got the call I thought, "Why not?"

ABOVE I always enjoy singing with symphonic orchestras. Here we are practising and sound-checking for the Dark Christmas concerts in Russia.

It is really fun to get together and do these big shows. Finns love Christmas and heavy metal and this is an event where the whole family can join in, grandparents and grandchildren alike. The Raskasta Joulua shows are very different from my own intimate Christmas concerts but they still require the same amount of preparation from me. Even if you are only singing five or six songs, it is a long show and you need to stay focused. I know other singers who have missed their slots because they have gone to the toilet or to smoke a cigarette! I have sung there with many other vocalists, including Tony Kakko from Sonata Arctica, and at the 2019 concerts, with Elize Ryd from Amaranthe and Dee Snider from Twisted Sister. I have also sung on one of the Raskasta Joulua albums, *Raskasta Joulua IV*, performing 'Ave Maria' with my old bandmate from Nightwish, Marco Hietala. I have the gold record of that on my wall.

In November 2020, an updated version of *From Spirits and Ghosts* was released. It featured the charity version of 'Feliz Navidad', as well as alternative recordings of 'Sublime Gracia' ('Amazing Grace'), 'Ô Viens, Ô Viens, Emmanuel' ('O Come, O Come, Emmanuel') and 'O Christmas Tree', along with a second disc entitled *Christmas Together: Live at Olomouc and Hradec Králové 2019*, which gave fans who hadn't been able to make my festive shows the opportunity to listen to what I had been doing since 2005. I really hope that, like my first Christmas album, *From Spirits and Ghosts* will become timeless and people will cherish it for years to come.

Finns love Christmas and heavy metal.

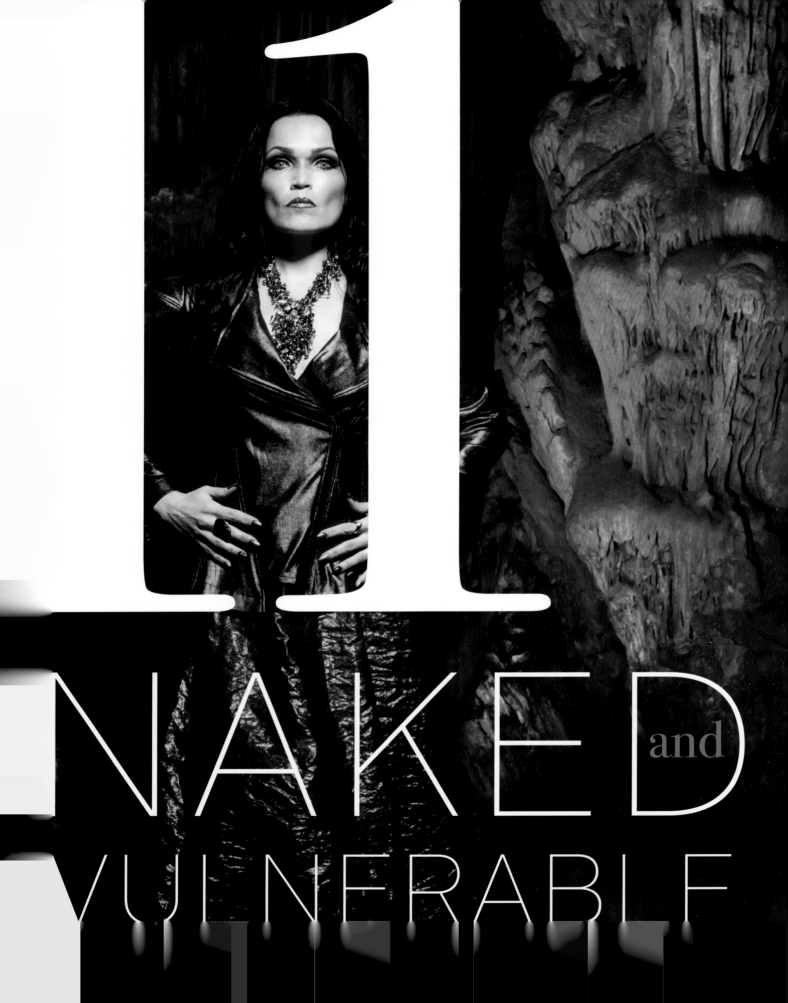

1

NAKED and

VULNERABLE

When the opening notes of 'Until My Last Breath' began, I started crying onstage. I was so happy to be alive. It was October 29, 2018 and the last date of my Nordic Symphony tour. Just one month earlier, I had suffered a stroke.

The morning of September 27 had begun like any other. I woke up and went to get my daughter her usual cup of milk, but something was wrong: I could not grasp the cup and it smashed to the floor. Marcelo called out to me, but I could not answer. I had lost the ability to speak, the left side of my face had dropped like it had melted, and the left-hand side of my body was completely numb. Thank God my husband realised what was happening and he rushed me to the hospital. The doctors discovered that I had a blood clot in my brain and they gave me an anti-coagulant injection to break it up. I had a very lucky escape and soon my speech and movement returned to normal, but I needed more tests and scans to find out what had caused it.

After three nights, I discharged myself from hospital so I could make the first night of the Nordic Symphony tour – I had 22 concerts booked in Europe. The doctors said to me, "No, señora, you're not going anywhere!" But I told them that the stress of cancelling my tour would end up killing me and it was true. I stand by my 'Die Alive' tattoo: if I was to die, it would be while being very much alive.

Having a stroke was such a huge shock because I was so fit and healthy. I kept asking myself how it could have happened to me. I just could not accept it and none of the doctors could give me an answer. Luckily, it was just a warning as no permanent damage was done, but it also made me realise just how close I had come to losing my voice and my ability to sing. It took me about a year to feel

confident in myself again. It made me realise just how fragile life is and that became the theme for *In the Raw*. Since the 1990s, I have been singing professionally and have learned much about my voice and what I am capable of doing. To sing classical music is a journey; it is not something you learn in one day, it is a never-ending process because your voice is constantly changing. When I began taking singing lessons, I sang in a very light soprano, but then when I learned about supporting my voice with my diaphragm, my voice got lower and my range reduced. That was around the time that Nightwish was born. So at the beginning of my professional music career, I was singing as a mezzo-soprano. Over the years, I have continued with my classical training and had several vocal coaches to help me.

There are hundreds of ways to sing and you have to find the best way for you that will not harm your voice. I had some singing students a few years ago and they would come to me with very difficult operas and I would say, "Why are you singing this song? You must know how to control your voice before pushing it to those dangerous levels." Even now, my voice is still not where I would love it to be. I would like to be able to hit the high notes better and not be so nervous about singing the more difficult parts of an aria, for example. I think a lot of this comes with age as much as it does with experience, as you tend to find that female classical singers start to shine after the age of 40.

ABOVE Taken on the last day of my tour with Stratovarius and Serpentyne. This tour was one of the nicest I have ever done.

OPPOSITE Timo asked me to powder his nose during our photo shoot in Finland. Sure, why not?

When it comes to rock singing, however, I no longer have those limitations. Now I compose my own songs, I tend to write two hard melodies for my vocals and, although the ranges are always pretty large, I know what I can handle. The melodies are still vocally demanding and I like the fact that not everyone can sing my songs. When I first joined Nightwish, I could not find many examples of singers who were combining lyrical vocals with metal, so I had to develop my own way of singing. In the early years, my voice got stuck in the back of my throat, but now it is brighter, lighter and I am back in the soprano range. It has taken years for me to feel comfortable, but I would say that started to happen around 2003, just before I began work on my first Christmas single, 'Yhden Enkelin Unelma'.

One of the most important things I have learned is that I need to take things a bit easier when I am on tour. I used to give 100 per cent in my performances, but now I have learned to only give 80 per cent – although nobody would notice. I have a microphone, so I do not need to push my voice as much, but it is difficult because it's so exciting to see the audience out there. I have learned to leave a couple of cookies in the jar so I do not use them all up during the show. It is about maintaining energy levels and, because I sing a lot on show days, on my days off, I keep quiet, I do not sing or talk too much or do interviews. If your body is tired, your voice is as well. And here is a very good opportunity for a disclaimer: I avoid interviews and promotion during my tours, so that my body can rest as much as possible when I am off stage. We can always do interviews before or after the tour, right? My main concern when on tour is to perform to the best of my abilities for my audience and for myself.

It is so important to stay as healthy as you can when you are a singer, both physically and mentally. Keeping fit and well is as important as vocal training for a lyrical singer like me. I cannot smoke or party or have just a couple of hours' sleep. My body is my instrument and it is super-important that I listen to what is going on with it. I have put my voice in danger in many different ways by singing in a loud metal band without being able to hear myself and not sleeping properly on tour, but my body has tried to keep up. It has not been the easiest road, but thankfully I have never had any major vocal issues since trying to sing those Whitney Houston songs when I was a young girl. I have learned some great breathing and vocal exercises that work well for me, but I know that different techniques work for different people as well. I still take singing lessons with a vocal coach when I feel the need.

> ❝
> # I like the fact that not everyone can sing my songs.

ABOVE Standing on books to correct my posture after I was struggling to relax my voice to record the vocals for *My Winter Storm*. This helped me breathe deeper and made me feel better. These days, I wear shoes with heels to achieve the same effect.

After recording the vocals on my first Christmas album, I remember telling myself: "If I ever record a classical album, this cannot be the way to do it." I have had to find the right way to record different songs myself. I realised I needed to work with my voice and to find out how to relax more.

My husband Marcelo and I have tried all sorts of tricks to help me feel more comfortable when I'm recording. For example, during the vocal recordings of *My Winter Storm*, when I was standing in a bad position, he stood me on a couple of books so that my heels were a little bit higher and I had a better posture.

My way of recording had already changed a lot by the time I recorded the album *Henkäys Ikuisuudesta* (Breath From Heaven) when we used the studio's biggest room and tried to find reflective surfaces that could be placed in front of me so my voice would vibrate more and give me feedback.

During this recording, I realised that I cannot wear headphones when recording classical vocals as they press against my jaw so I cannot fully open my mouth. Instead, I sang with one headphone off, and sometimes I would leave the headphones nearby just to listen to the music coming out of them like from a small radio. It was such a painful experience on Schubert's 'Ave Maria', though, because if I do not hear my natural voice when I am singing classical, I find it very difficult to project.

I do sometimes use headphones for recording rock songs where I do not need to use so much of my lyrical technique. I can also sing pop songs while wearing headphones and I wear them to record backing vocals and harmonies that I usually use on my records – otherwise it would be impossible – but I needed to develop a way to record vocals without headphones. Nowadays, I use a monitor speaker with the music at a low volume right in front of the microphone. I sing and do live takes without any headphones so I can hear my natural voice and feel comfortable. That was the way I recorded *My Winter Storm*, too. No recording engineer or mixing engineer has ever said to me, "You cannot record like that."

I am always very interested to hear how other people record and how they relax during the process because it is never a truly laidback environment. Rock singers, such as Epica's Simone Simons and Lacuna Coil's Cristina Scabbia, for example, agree with me that the headphones never make your voice sound natural, so you have to adapt to the situation. Tim Palmer once told me that when he recorded with U2, their singer Bono was singing next to him into a handheld microphone. You have to find what is right for you, which is something I have thankfully done.

I recorded no more than two or three songs a day during those sessions – which was about the same as I had done with Nightwish. However, with the band I

RIGHT Julian is always there to help me with my demos and any issues I might have with them, but this time he ended up recording my vocals for *In the Raw* as well. Here I am getting ready to record some keyboard parts.

BELOW Recording without headphones means I can hear my voice properly. Also, it makes me more relaxed, meaning I'm not restrained when singing the more vocally demanding parts.

Alex Scholpp, guitars

"I've had so many favourite moments with Tarja. I love the times in the studio, working long hours and getting results are fantastic for me because I love to work on songs and record parts. Touring the world with Tarja and getting to play all these amazing places has also been a blessing. Every band and artist has their own life and magic onstage and I have to say that Tarja kills it every night. She's a total pro, even when she has a cold or jet lag; when it's showtime, she's there 150 per cent, which makes my job easy. I've always loved playing with her and I see my role as to play as tight and in tune as possible so she can feel good singing onstage.

"I was originally booked as a session guitar player, along with Doug Wimbish on bass and Earl Harvin on drums, to record *My Winter Storm* at Grouse Lodge Studio in Ireland. The idea was that we would play as a band and Tarja, Marcelo and Daniel Presley would re-arrange and produce. We'd then take a break, play it again differently and see what happened.

"I was writing guitar parts in one room while the drums and bass were being recorded in another, so that we had more options to choose from, and we went from there. It was really fun and we were especially creative as a group. It was during this session that Tarja asked me to provide some song ideas which became 'Ciaran's Well'. Afterwards, she asked if I would also like to play in her live band. I remember her saying: 'What are your plans for the next two years?' Those two years have turned into 14 and counting!

"From that very first recording, we developed a good relationship and it grew from there. I think there's been at least one song on every album that we've written together besides writing and recording the guitar parts.

"We recorded *What Lies Beneath* in Finland during the winter and there was such a great atmosphere. Outside it was cold and there was so much snow, but we all stayed together in one house. *Colours in the Dark* was recorded in a studio in Buenos Aires and after that I recorded the guitars at my place. We've shared so many studio experiences and been on the road for such a long time that we've developed a really good understanding of the way each other works. It's really important to me to be there to help Tarja get to where she wants to be with the music.

"Tarja has grown over the years as an artist and songwriter, both onstage and in the studio, but she's still exactly the same person underneath as when I first met her in Ireland. She's always been totally professional and prepared to work extremely hard. I've only met a few other people that are that strong and focused on their goals. She's Tarja and she'll always be a very special person, a very special artist and she can't be compared to anyone else. Over the years, it feels like we've grown into a big family. I've been playing in her band for 14 years now, which is the longest time I've ever played in a band. It's crazy how time flies."

did a lot of backing vocals, while this was more straight-forward singing – very demanding and very different. *Henkäys Ikuisuudesta* is the last album for which I recorded all of the vocals in a proper studio. It inspired me to get away from dampened rooms and find a place that would suit my big voice. The first vocal recordings for *My Winter Storm* were done in a rented house in Ibiza and we were there for a month with the producer. Since then I have always recorded vocals in a home studio that's been prepared for me, whether in Finland, Argentina, Antigua or Spain. The place is very important because I want to feel relaxed and not have to check the clock all the time. I used a recording engineer for my vocal recording sessions for many years and still do, but things have evolved so much that eventually I would be recording on my own sometimes.

Now during the recording process, I am calmer and my voice sounds stronger and more certain. You can definitely hear that on *In the Raw*. It is a very personal album, so I really had to go for it without any fear and it felt good.

When I first began work on the album, I had no idea I would be writing such intimate lyrics. I started gathering material and going through my archives during the *Shadow Self* album tour. At the time, I was listening to a lot of guitar-based bands and that is where a lot of my musical inspiration came from. I do not like happy, very orchestrated heavy metal; I am more into basic guitar-riffing and that organic sound was what I was looking for. My guitarist Alex wrote the first songs in this way and I fell in love with the demos. They sounded so raw and that is where the idea for the title came from. Usually when you record guitars, you layer up six tracks – sometimes even more than that – to make it sound powerful, but I said to Alex, "Only play two tracks of guitars, they're sounding really good that way." Instead of beginning the process with one of my piano demos, I gave Alex directions for 'Dead Promises' and 'Goodbye Stranger' and then I could shape the melodies and the lyrics myself. I wanted these songs to have a more vintage sound and to capture the energy of our live shows.

On this album, I really wanted to take control and I wrote most of the lyrics on my own to find out if I was capable of doing that. I had already begun writing the first songs before my stroke and I put the finishing touches to them just a few months afterwards, in January 2019. It was a very difficult process because many of the songs are so personal. I remember sitting on my couch in front of a blank screen, thinking: "I'm going to do this." I needed to encourage myself and be brave. I am the most critical person when it comes to my work, but afterwards I read my lyrics and I knew I could be proud of them. I remember the last song I wrote was 'Shadow Play' and when I finished it I almost cried with happiness. My stroke had made me feel vulnerable and I did not want to be weak: I am a fighter and I decided that I was going to conquer my fears.

My stroke was not the only personal issue that took place during this period. Many tragic things happened within my extended family, too. There is a lot of personal stuff on the album and getting them out of my system through music was such a spiritually cleansing process. We artists are very lucky that we have this outlet. Singing these songs live is different, though, because in a way they have already lived their life and no longer hold the same power for me. But of course I remember how it felt when I was writing them.

The album title was also a direct response to the themes on the album. I had found myself in the raw and when I discovered that gold is a raw element, it got me thinking about the artwork. Gold is an elegant metal and a lot of people treasure it, but as I continued researching the topic I got to thinking about how molten metal in meteorites hitting the earth millions of years ago had brought gold to the centre of the Earth, and felt that that connected to the music: there is both heaviness and sophistication on the album but they are in harmony. It takes you on a journey from pure metal to that sophisticated golden chamber. It all fitted together.

I recorded the vocals at home in Spain and the rest of the guys recorded at their different locations. It was the first studio album that my current live drummer Timm Schreiner appears on – but he doesn't even need a click track; he is perfect! I felt like the band's playing

There is a lot of **personal stuff** on the album and getting them out of my system through music was such a **spiritually cleansing process.**

supported my voice just as it does onstage and that is why some songs – such as 'Goodbye Stranger' – only contain drums, guitar, bass and vocals. There is also a little less orchestra and keyboard compared to previous releases.

It felt different working on the mixes with Tim Palmer because I was not there with him in the studio this time. I really pushed him to make the songs sound heavier than before and I remember sending him examples of songs by Five Finger Death Punch, In Flames and even Disturbed. He said to me, "This is very interesting that you're progressing, you're going further." He said he really liked that I was pushing him to change as well.

ABOVE I got to meet Tommy Karevik in Spain a few years ago during a festival. He had just recorded vocals for my *In the Raw* album, so it was really nice to meet him in person to show him my gratitude.

I really wanted to have some duets on the album but did not write any of the songs with a second voice in mind. However, it was during the recording process that I started to realise that some songs could work in that way. I wanted to celebrate my metal sisterhood with Cristina Scabbia on 'Goodbye Stranger'. I have always been a big fan of Kamelot's Tommy Karevik and Soilwork's Björn Strid although I had never met either of them. They are both good, emotional singers so I dared to ask them if they would sing with me on *In the Raw*. With Björn, I wanted a singer that could growl and sing with clean vocals – thankfully he liked the idea. In Tommy's case, I wanted him to partner me with clean, emotional vocals – he delivered about 40 tracks of vocals that made me cry because they were so beautiful.

My love of Paulo Coelho's literary work inspired 'Railroads'. I wrote the music to that a long time ago, possibly even around the time of *What Lies Beneath*, but there were no lyrics for it then. You can hear that original demo on the *Extra Raw* edition of the album. My lyrical inspiration came from Paulo's book *Aleph* (2011), in which he takes the Trans-Siberian Express through Russia and details his spiritual experiences on the journey. My own amazing, colourful journey in life feels like a rollercoaster, so it worked perfectly. (I have never travelled on the Trans-Siberian Express, but it is on my bucket list.)

'You and I' is a tribute to all those great ballads of the 70s and 80s. Nobody writes those kinds of songs any more, so I wanted to make one of my own and use the piano, which is such an emotional instrument. We also recorded a full-band version of the song which also forms part of *Extra Raw*. I wrote the lyrics for it with Mathias, who co-wrote 'I Walk Alone' right at the beginning of my solo story. It is about relationships in general and how complicated they can be, but also how easy. I have been so lucky in my marriage to Marcelo in that respect because we have a lot of understanding for each other. I recorded the piano at home, which was a super-relaxed experience. Recording an instrument to me is more nerve-wracking than recording the vocals because it is an extension of my body, so I cannot control it in the same way. I always enjoy playing piano during my shows and it is a skill I want to maintain.

After *From Spirits and Ghosts*, I welcomed Jim onto my rock albums once again. He has played a big role for me as orchestra arranger and composer ('Deliverance' was written with him). I told him that I wanted to score a song without any guitars or drums and asked him to give me the first idea for it. That became 'The Golden Chamber'. He sent me some tracks from which I could choose the beginning and I used the masterful *Once Upon a Time in the West* theme, by film music maestro Ennio Morricone, as inspiration for the middle part. I even recorded a demo with his melody as a guiding track for Jim to work on. I also added my own Finnish language section in between; I felt I wanted to return to writing Finnish lyrics as I had not written a full song in my mother tongue since 'Oasis' on my first rock album.

I always keep everything we record during the sessions and think it's really nice to produce special editions with these tracks on so fans have something else to listen to. We included an alternative percussion mix of 'Spirits of the Sea' with the Brazilian percussionist Carlinhos Brown on *Extra Raw*. He is very famous in Brazil and was also a coach on the local version of *The Voice*, so that was something we had in common. I thought it would be wonderful to have a version with a lot more percussion on 'Spirits of the Sea' because it is such a cinematic song. He played an amazing number of tracks that could not be heard on the album version, and I wanted them to have their own life because his work is amazing.

In the Raw was released on August 30, 2019 and the first part of the *Raw* tour was in South America that September. We had a great time and it was very successful. We had a break and were due to head off on a tour of Europe in March 2020 when we started to hear about a new virus that was beginning to spread around the world. It was a flashback to visiting Mexico during the 2009 *Storm* tour when swine flu was hitting the country. I remember my fans turning up to see shows wearing face masks, which they had decorated with Tarja logos and designs. It was really strange: I could not hug them or even shake hands. Now it seemed to be happening again.

In March 2020, no one realised just how serious the situation would become, but we had dates booked and tickets had been sold, so we decided to go ahead with the tour. I had a meeting with my crew and we agreed to take the precautions that were being recommended by the World Health Organization: we were washing our hands more often and for longer than usual, we had alcohol hand sanitiser everywhere and we agreed that we would practise social distancing with people outside our tour bus. In the end, we played four shows: one in Portugal and three in Spain. Gigs were already starting to get cancelled along the way, but we drove into Marseilles, France, on March 13. The crew had been working their asses off since that morning and we were about to do a soundcheck when the venue announced they would be suspending the gig due to the virus. My fans were waiting outside for the meet and greet so I went out to see them. It was so sad. People were crying and it felt really awkward that we could not do the show. I needed to make a tough decision and finish the tour there. We all made our way back home and I only just made it back in time before the Spanish government closed the borders. It was such a relief when I finally got to see Naomi and Marcelo and we all quarantined together at home. Thankfully everyone in my crew was OK, and they all got home safely, but it was a very strange time.

Life in lockdown was a great challenge. A lot of people might think it would have provided me with the perfect opportunity to get creative, but at first I was simply in shock. There was a lot to think about but, little by little, my inspiration began to return. I found myself enjoying being with my family even more and it was wonderful to see my daughter happy to have me at home, but she told me, "It's been amazing to have you home but I also know how much you miss and love your work." And that is exactly how I felt, but it also gave me the chance to explore new ways of connecting with my fans on social media. I wanted to offer some light relief in the form of live performances and interviews, but I still felt so much uncertainty over the situation. How long would it take

ABOVE Kippis! Our visit to a tequila factory in Mexico. It was very interesting to learn about the history of this legendary drink.

OPPOSITE In 2009, I did a show in Mexico City where swine flu had just broken out. One of my fans gave me this mask, and now I look at it, it connects me with our current reality with COVID-19.

BELOW I really love the enthusiasm of my fans who wait for me outside the concert venues. This photo was taken during the *Colours in the Dark* tour. I promised to meet them after my soundcheck was done in Lille, France.

for concerts to return to normal? Nobody knew, so I started to think of other ways to occupy myself.

I have never been addicted to social media, but I enjoy using it. Facebook is for important announcements, I use Twitter to describe how I feel in that moment, and Instagram is for funny or nice pictures. I love photography and checking out what other people are shooting. I think it is important to give my fans a glimpse of the real person behind the art and it is unbelievable how many followers I have. And yes, I do write my own posts on social media, although my assistant handles some of the more official ones for tour dates and releases.

Coronavirus could not stop me making plans for the future, of course. I quickly gave up on feeling frustrated by the restrictions of the pandemic; you cannot fight against the universe, you have to stay positive, find new ways to be inspired and continue with your art.

*t*orsten and I began writing together in Antigua after *My Winter Storm* and in 2010 we decided to create an unusual project together. He is an electronic music producer and, around the time we were recording *What Lies Beneath*, I wrote a song that I wanted him to put his electronic stamp on. It was called 'Outlanders' and we previewed it online in 2011. The lyrics are taken from the Finnish language translation of Paulo Coelho's text – I had not been in contact with him by this point and had to ask his Finnish publisher for permission to use it. They put me in direct contact and when I saw his first email in my inbox, I freaked out! I am such a huge fan and we have stayed in touch ever since.

I remember the producer Daniel Presley once telling me that I should sample my voice. I love working on vocal arrangements – backing vocals, harmonies, choirs and using my voice like an instrument – and it was something that I thought could be interesting to do. For this project, my mind was made up: I didn't want to use my voice only as a conventional soloist in the song; I also wanted to use it as an instrument.

From this idea grew a project which we named after my song. I am an outlander because I am not living in my home country and Torsten is also an outlander because he is German but living in Antigua. Brazilian Paulo Coelho has his residence in Switzerland, and I had an idea to involve a guitar player as I wanted the project to be based on vocals, electronic music and guitars. These three elements are a constant in all the songs and are equally important.

2009

THIS PAGE Here you can see how many years Torsten and I have spent working on *Outlanders* – these photos have been taken over 10 years. It has been a very rewarding and enjoyable, stress-free project.

2013

2014

2015

2019

LET'S NOT LEAVE
IT HERE, LET'S
START WRITING
MORE MUSIC

PREVIOUS PAGE Many years ago, we filmed the video for the song 'Outlanders' in Antigua. I was pregnant at the time and deeply enjoyed the shoot, because I could simply gaze at the island's beautiful landscape.

BELOW Shooting the video for 'Outlanders' with Tim Tronckoe on the coast of Marbella, Spain.

The first guitar player I approached was Walter Giardino. He is from the band Rata Blanca and is a very famous rock guitar player in Argentina with a sort of 70s Deep Purple/Rainbow sound. We have been friends for ages and we always joke about the fact that, if Walter had been born in the UK or USA, he would probably be listed as one of the greatest guitarists ever. I completely believe that, and, of course, he is also another outlander living abroad. He had never worked on an electronic project before, but he was open-minded about doing it.

That was where it started, and I said to Torsten, "Let's not leave it here, let's start writing more music."

Ever since, we have been writing together in Antigua. We created 12 songs for the album, with videos to accompany some of them. Four were new versions of Torsten´s or my solo songs and six were brand-new tracks, mostly inspired by Antigua, including 'Cruelest Goodbye', 'Echoes', '1971' and 'Closer to the Sky'. I did 'Cruelest Goodbye' with the Swedish songwriter Harry Sommerdahl, who co-wrote 'I Walk Alone'. There was also a cover of Depeche Mode's 'World In My Eyes' on which I sing in such a low register you wouldn't recognise my voice. There was also a new version of 'Never Too Far' with Mike Oldfield, and the album features some very famous guitar players including Al di Meola, Vernon Reid (from Living Colour), Joe Satriani and Steve Rothery from Marillion, who plays on a new version of 'Mystique Voyage'. The guitarists all have a unique style and sound, which enhances the mood of each song. They are all virtuoso players and they add acoustic and electric guitar to these beautiful melodies. It is absolutely amazing how well the electronic music merges with it. It is a completely different world from my rock and classical music, and it was wonderful to work on. The music is very chilled, very relaxed and allowed me to experiment with my voice and express myself differently. Music is about emotions and I wanted to show myself in a different light with this project. Some day I would love to take *Outlanders* on the road.

RIGHT My friend, Argentinean guitarist Walter Giardino, and me, after recording a few songs for the electronic project *Outlanders* in Buenos Aires. Although Walter is a very well-known guitar player in rock, he embarked on this adventure without any preconceptions and did an amazing job.

ESPECIALLY FOR THE METAL QUEEN!
YOUR WORK IS A GIFT, AND YOU DESERVE TO BE
CROWNED!
BRAZIL LOVES YOU, QUEEN!

TARJA TURUNEN

epilogue

Hello, Old Friend

My stage outfits hang on rails in my garage. They sparkle and shimmer under strip lighting, ready for my next performance, but since March 2020, they have been gathering dust. I often go down there to enjoy the striking colours and elegant materials of my classical gowns. Among them is a beautiful turquoise silk dress that Marcelo bought for me many years ago; I wore it during the first Noche Escandinava shows in 2001 and memories of those performances come flooding back as I lift the protective plastic to admire what lies beneath.

Over this past year, I have felt like a trapped butterfly. I have really missed playing concerts and meeting all my beautiful fans; I have had an amazing journey so far and there is still so much more to come. I have found my muse again and have so many ideas for the future. Our lives might feel suspended like the dust circling my stage wear, but I will never stop dreaming and I will fight as hard as I can to share my dreams with you.

I am ready, are you?

OPPOSITE I have received hundreds of gifts from fans during my career and I keep most of them at home. It is so amazing to see the talent and originality that has gone into them.

discography

ALBUMS

NOCHE ESCANDINAVA II, a Finnish Evening from Buenos Aires, April 24th, 2004 (2005)

CD

HENKÄYS IKUISUUDESTA – BREATH FROM HEAVEN (2006)

CD Finland   CD Argentina   LP   Jouluinen Platinapainos (2010)

MY WINTER STORM (2007)

CD / LP   CD + Bonus DVD   2CD Extended Special Edition (2008)

SINGLES / EP

Yhden Enkelin Unelma – One Angel's Dream

CD Finland   CD Acoustic Finland   CD EP Finland   CD EP Argentina

You Would Have Loved This

CD

I Walk Alone

CD 2 Tracks   Single Cut   Artist Cut

Die Alive   The Seer EP   Enough

CD   CD / LP   Digital Only

Maailman Kauneimmat Joululaulut

CD

ALBUMS

WHAT LIES BENEATH (2010)

CD / CD 14 Tracks / CD + DVD 2CD Deluxe Version USA Japan

Dreamer's Box Set

TARJA TURUNEN & HARUS – IN CONCERT LIVE AT SIBELIUS HALL (2011)

CD / CD + DVD DVD / DVD + CD / Blu-ray + CD

ACT I (2012)

2CD LP DVD Blu-ray

Mediabook

COLOURS IN THE DARK (2013)

CD CD Special Limited Edition LP Box Set

BEAUTY & THE BEAT Tarja Turunen & Mike Terrana (2014)

2CD DVD / Blu-ray

SINGLES / EP

Falling Awake   CD / 7" Vinyl / 10"Vinyl

I Feel Immortal   CD

Until My Last Breath   CD

Underneath

Digital 7" Vinyl

Walking in the Air – Live

Digital Only

Into The Sun (Radio Edit) (Live)

Digital Only

Never Enough Digital Only

Victim Of Ritual   CD / 7" Vinyl

500 Letters   Digital Only

ALBUMS

LEFT IN THE DARK (2014)

CD / LP

LUNA PARK RIDE (2015)

2CD LP DVD / Blu-ray

AVE MARIA – EN PLEIN AIR (2015)

CD LP Digital

THE BRIGHTEST VOID (2016)

CD LP / Digital

THE SHADOW SELF (2016)

CD / CD + DVD LP / Digital Limited Box Set

FROM SPIRITS AND GHOSTS (Score for a Dark Christmas) (2017)

CD LP Digital Box Set

SINGLES / EP

Never Enough (Live)

Digital Only

No Bitter End

7" Vinyl + CD

An Empty Dream

CD

Innocence

7" Vinyl + CD CD (MH)

Demons In You

CD

O Come, O Come, Emmanuel

7" Vinyl

O Tannenbaum

7" Vinyl

Feliz Navidad

7" Vinyl

Fsag – Dark Versions

Digital Only

ALBUMS

ACT II (2018)

2CD   Digital   LP   DVD / Blu-ray

 Mediabook

IN THE RAW (2019)

CD / Digital   LP   Box Set

EXTRA RAW (2020)

CD (Exclusive to ITR Box Set) / Digital

CHRISTMAS TOGETHER: Live at Olomouc and Hradec Králové 2019 (2020)

LP

FROM SPIRITS AND GHOSTS (Score for a Dark Christmas) (2020)

2CD (Including Christmas Together)

SINGLES / EP

Love to Hate (Live in London)

Digital Only

Undertaker (Live in Milan)

Digital Only

Victim of Ritual (Live at Woodstock)

Digital Only

Dead Promises

Digital Only

Railroads

Digital Only

Tears In Rain

Digital Only

You and I

Digital Only

Together (Live at Hradec Králové 2019)

Digital Only

Have Yourself a Merry Little Christmas (Live at Hradec Králové 2019)

Digital Only

roll of honour

The publishers gratefully acknowledge the contribution of everyone listed below, whose generous support helped bring this project to fruition.

Nicole A

Lorena Aal

Sami Aaltonen

Vanessa Aaslepp

Leonides Abarca

Jose Alberto Flores Acevedo

Caylyn Adamko

Maciek Aduckiewicz

Timo Ahde

Jalal Ahmed

Fahad Al Suwaidi

Alex & Hanna

Danilo Alfarone

Christina Algate

Gunilla Algotsson

Alina

Lance Allan Hill

Chiara Allasia

Douglas de Almeida

Altariel

José Rodríguez Álvarez

Liza Álvarez Fernández

Peter Anders

Vincze András

Karla Angelica

Matthew Angelo

Angi

Annelien

America Arana

Ricardo Arana

Jeroni Araque Gimenez

Brenda Avijail George Arroyo

Christopher Arsenault

Elodie Artour

John Aston

Ben Atkinson

Babs Avila

Phil B.

Cody Bachman

Sean Bahan

Joanne Bain

Filipa Barbosa

Daniela Barbulescu

Katrin Bardtke

Subhadeep Barman

David Barron

Larissa Barth

Sara Batllori

James A. Bauer Sr.

Melanie Bebak

Brian Becker

Rob Beedy

Georg Bege

Ramona Beijer

Thomas A. Bellis

Martina Benesova

Gibeaux Benoist

Heather Berthereau

Cony Betz

Alessio Biancardo

Marcelo Biaso

Tanja Bienmüller

Steven L. Bigalk

Jason Birch (Evanwishcoil)

Dirk Bittermann

Barbara Blackthorne

Lisa Bodem

Remon Boegman

Jody Boettinger

Esther Bogaart Soethoudt

Valerie Bollinger

Serhiy Bondarev

Judith Bonifer

Patrick Borner

Bartosz Bosko

Rémi Bournisien

Josué Boutineau

Carola Bouwdewijns

Matthew J. Bowen

Amanda Bozuwa

Carlo Bozzetta

Kate Brandt

Zdena Brandysova

Tanja Braun

Gustavo Diaz Bregolin

Anaelle Brenner

Polo Breschi

Leigh Broschat

Andrew Broxham

The Brueland Family

Rena Brunhofer

Rocìo Buccoliero

Buraddori

Virginia Butler

Steve Butty Butterworth

Ann C.

Lurdes Caldeira

Laura Calliauw

Sandra Calloch

Rocio Calvillo Sampedro

Maz Cameron

Stefano Campanella

René Camplair

Irene Canziani

Irwin Raudel Cárdenas
Amezquita

Estephanie A. Cardoso

Patrizia Carimati

Will Carrero

Scot Cash

Jennifer Casselman
and Adam Brookhouse

Gianluigi Castiglioni

Margherita Cattaneo

Serena Cavina

Mara Celegato

Václav Červinka

David Chacón

Zangelica Chaffee

Nikos Cheilakis

Brian Chen

Dave Chidwick

Patsaki Christina

Kenneth J. Chun

Carla Cilvik

Jeffrey Clark

Jessica Clingempeel

Kevin Coadou

Scott D. Coe

Scott D. Coe

Ton Coenen

Elizabeth Cole

Nasi Coll

Bill Conn

Jessica Connelly

Adam Cook

Joseph L. Coon

Serge Coriandoli

Amy Corkery

Sandy Cormier

Cosette

Zaid Couri

Sean Cowie

Silviu Craciun

Mike Crane

Luís Miguel Cravo Rodrigues

Mac Cremer

Valentina Crescentini

Myla Cruz

Daniela Cunha

Chris Cunniffe

Colin Cunningham

Dawn Curry

Freddy Soca Cutti

Magdalena Czyżykowska

D'iane

Yulai Danieli

DanyD

Darkrain

Charles Davidson

Oriana Davila (Naiad of Winter)

Douglas de Almeida

Eliane De Almeida

Chris De Houwer

Fernando de la Maza

Rodrigo De Vincenzo Monteiro

Ron de Vries

Jeff Deboo

Suzanne DeCree

Danique Dellevoet

Katie DelliSanti

Wolfgang Demmler

Lily Deniel

Viki Dĕtinská

Craig Devlin

Vladimir Diaconescu

Ana Paula Díaz

Zoe Dickinson

Luis Diego

Victoria S. Dieste

Alena Dintyu

Andrey Dmitriev

Rob Dobisch

Ariadna Doicescu

Darklings Doll

Pablo Donoso

Kiss Dóra

Doreen

Adrian Dorin Șerbănică

Dörthe

David Doshi

Marga Dovgal

Nadine Drakon

Gavrila Dreve

Nicky Dundas

Vee Dunne

Clíona Duwe

Erika E

Svenja E

Yvonne Ebner

Dave Edwards

Marthe Eeckhout

Wianne Eilers

Sarah Elizabeth Wilson

Chris Ellaway

Owain Thomas Ellis

Hannu Elmeri Ojala

David Elvin

Denny Engel

Jacques Engler

Lance Erichsen

Daphne Erickson

George Erkekoglou

Maaike Essenstam

Emily Estilow

Wendy Estrada-Andrade

Aleksandar Evtimov

Sabrina Liliana Fabris

Metzgerei Fackiner

Silvio Falb

Marcel Faßbender

Andrea Fatér

Lukas Schölzel

Maxence Fauconnier

Michell & Sarah Fehr

Anika Felkel

Mira Feng

Roberta Danielle Pilot Ferguson

Isabel Fernández Rodríguez

Rick Ferrero

Laura Ferroni

Edwardo Fielding

Cristina Fiorido

Massimo Fiorino

Christian Flack

Mickaël Flandrin

Noémie Foare

Frankie Formosa

Shanell Foskey

Mic Fowkes

Tim Fox

Fina Foxy

Frances and Alexis

Ruud Franken

Charlotte Frese

Thomas Fritsch

Agatha Fuentes Frez

Janna Fung

Andrea Corpas Gallardo

Tatyana Ganus

Yesenia Garcia

Antonio Garcia

Anne-Charlotte Garsin

Thomas Moro Gasparini

Kathleen Gebhart

David Gentry

Liza Georjon

Cenan Gercekci

Bianca Gerschitz

Sara Giacometti

Madeline Gibard

Dylan Gibson

Chloe Gilholy

David Gill

Noémie Gillet

Bill Gilmour

Zach Gingrich

Ilaria Giombelli

David Giroux

Gary Glowacki

Mina-Ly Godin

Ted Gola

Chris, Crystal & Ziggy Golightly

Ryszard Golla

Nathalie Göller

Gille Gomand

Franklin Goncalves

Fabio Cesar Gonzalez

Jerry Gonzalez

J. Humberto González M.

Cécile Goujon

Clementine Govaert

Steven van Graafeiland

Elio Grassivaro

Pat Gravino

Ian Greenfield

Ethelwen Greenleaf

Marc Gregory

Katherine Grey

Xionary Guerrero

Maylin Guida

Basak Günel

Cav Robert John Gunn KGO.

Nanna Gustafsson

Roberto Gutiérrez Adones

Luis Guzman

Sanneke H.

Karina Assis Haddad

Torbjørn Håland

Shannon Hale

Tria Hall

Monica Hamilton

Stuart Hamilton

Mandy Handforth

Hanka

Martin Hans

Linn Hansson

Franziska Noelle Harbers

Jack Hardy

Holger Hartstein

Bianca Hassemer

Konstantin Hayat

Adam Hearn

Mia Hed

Sina Heidenreich

Heidi from CZ

Anne Heinänen

Andreas Heinisch

Frances Heinrich-Krüger

Sarah Heinzig

Marijana Henezi

Charles Herbert

Julia Hermann

Roger Hermansson

Steven Herrmann

Zachary Hewitt

Ben Hipperson

Alan Hiscocks

Namiko Hitotsubashi

Sabrina Hobbie

Debra Holden

Gabriela Hollman-Borg

Randy Holmberg

Homeira

Didier Honoré

Niall Hope (fester112)

Sarina Hoppe

Gen»õiana Horodnic

Emma Houlton

Glenn Howells

Valerie Hudak

Siobhan 'Siony' Hudson

Adrian Huggins

Anthony Hughes

Mira Huhtaniemi

Sandra Hupková

Caroline Huselstein

Anna i Bogdan

Andrei Ilin

Dmitry Ivankov

Milena Ivy

Marjo J

Pascal J

Ivan Jacquin

André Jäger

Stefan Janjic

Heidi Jankola

Marc Jansen

Jaroslav Jedlička

Jelena & Victor

Ana Jelifá

Paul Jessop

Arjen 'Ayreon' Jimmink

Claudia Jirkuff

Ladislav Jiterský

Stian Johnsen

Mark Johnson

Neil Johnston

Mélanie Jolly

Andrew Jones

Roger Jones

Joseba

Tato Miranda (Josenilson)

Alice Junier

Iiris Juntunen

Riku & Hannu Juutilainen

Kai-Uwe

Markus Kanerva

Anna-Maija Karppinen

Andrik-Csutak Katalin

Brian Kelman

Amy Kempen

Stefani Keogh

Mario Kezman Mac

Shannen L.C. Khare

Yan Khilkevich

Simon James King

Gisel Kingston

Gabriela Kisova

Miroslav Kitler

Andrew Klaus

Alexander Klein

Ștefan Klemisch

Vojtěch Kliment

Lukáš Klinovský

Maximilian Knapke

Jasmina Knežić Ćumo

Hannes Kniepeis

Jessica Knoll

Caroline Knoth

Ian Knowles

Kevin Koblischke

Max, Ian, Lorís, Edwin Koehn

Claudio Köhl

George J Kokonas

Sandra Könemann

Anna Kopuletá

Christine Kosar

Damian Kosz

Jillian Kovach

Steffen Kowal

Eva Kozáková

Christian Kremer

Sabrina Kreuzer

Karsai Krisztián

Bianka Krisztina Nagy

Leo J. Kryger

Rainer Krystek

Aleksi Kuivalainen

Daniel Kumar

Sara la Fontaine

Lynn Laaksonen

Stefanie Lades

Joselyn Lago

Stéphane Lagrevol

Sami Lahtinen

Mika Laitinen

Sylvia Lambrecht

David C. LaMendola

Dr. Carolin Maria Lang-Groß

Karin Laumann

Céline Le Vu

Valentin Lécuyer

Patricio Contreras Ledezma

Audrey Lee

Kristy Lee

Aaron Leeder

Katherine Leon

Alessandra Leoni

Karen LeRoy

Wojtek Lesniewicz

Marek Lesniowski

Sebastien Leyris

Christina Liebig

Floor Lips

Mariusz Lis

Berenice Hernandez Lomas

Valerie Long

Victoria Long

Andrii Loshkovskyi

Michael Löv

Line Iren Løvvig

Eddie Lowe

Richard Lowe

Enrique Loyola Martínez

Joaquim Roberto Pinto Ferraz
Luz Junior

Kai Määttä

Scott MacFarlane

Boglárka Mácová

Jorge Madeira

Christophe Magat

Maggie Magnoire Collins

Lars Maibach

Mélanie Maigret

Francisco Maiquez Solorzano

Melissa Maloch

Matti Manninen

Alfredo Alba Mansilla

Jakub Marcinkowski

Marosvölgyi Márkó

Susana C. Marquez

Martin

Pedro Silvestre Martín

Marlyn Martinez

Patricio Martínez

Gaëtan Massin

Ioana Mateescu

Mateusz

Vanessa Roschel Matos

Mikael Mattsson

Anthony May

Laura Mazard

Dariusz Mazurek

Phil McCartney

Becky McIntosh

James McLaren

Simon Edward McMurdo

Michel Mdjay

Alexandra Mehesz

Gavin Meiklejohn

Gavin Meiklejohn

Kerstin Meissler

Sophia-Theresa Melahn

Dennis Meldhedegaard-Nielsen

Shirley B. Mello

Dalvan F. Meloni

Antonio Mendez

Uwe Merkelbach

Emiliano Mezzadri

Lord Alex Miller

Scott Miller

Miroslav Minárik

Robert Minderhoud

Matthias Mintel

Peter Mitchell

Andreas Möller

Monika Wittwer

Axel de Montalembert

Chip Moody

Moonemy

Jessica Moorlag

Michaela Moravcova

Morganna

Joyce Morin

Ana Moronta

Ann Moutrey

Scotch Mowery

Peter Munsters

Ryan Murray

Carla Murray

Peter Nagy

Jeanine Nahkala

Kevin Naiad

Josep Navarra Artigas

Andreea Neamtu

Talles Neiva

Tímea Németh

Simone Netwen

Heiko Neumann

Elisabeth Marie Tarja Nielsen

Tero Nieminen

Ambra Nihil

Richard Nodesjö

Ligeia Noire

Saskia Noordzij

Monika Howard & Norris

Sabrina Norton

Ondřej Novák

Carla Nuñez

Olivia Nuret

Klaus Oetter

Ana Luiza de Oliveira

Sonia Oliveira

Oneirica

Alejandra Camus Ordenes

Agneta Östling

Ghislain Ouellet

Carlos Pacheco

Corinne Padilla

Wayne J. Paine

Stefanie Pakulla

Joseph Pallozzi

Michael Palmer

Ioana Pandele

Mariel Parada

Alfonso Páramo Gómez

Veronica Paratico

Chris & Debbie Parsons

Patricia

T. S. Pedersen

Leevi Pekanmäki

Tuuli Pennanen

Linnea Perbjörs

José Antonio Pérez Rodríguez

Leandro Pettino

Nicolas Peyrat

Gavin Phillips

Ellis Phoenix

Graham Pierce

Priscilla I. Pinales

Luis Pineda

Manuel Cuenca Piñero

Geraldo Pinho

Rejane Pissurno

Cas Pleijsier

Irma Ploeger

Vladimir Podborsky

Joe Polizzi

Kimmo Pollari

Gaëlle Pongerard

Latasha Renea Poole

Les Poole

Angelique W. Poppaea

Hagen Poppitz

Adrián Posada Rey

Yrjan Post

Nancy Powell

Michal Praj

Franziska Preuss

Martin Pribula

David Price

Scott "Scott Free" Proce

Roy Quesenberry

Raul Quezada

Laura R

Rachel R

Pamela Ramos

Patricia Rangel

Joonas Rasinen

Nadja Rautiainen

Topi Rautiainen

Raven

Tana Ray

James Read

Colin Reed

Markus and Viktoriya Regele

Laura Regreny

Anke Reich

Cassandra Reiß

Andreas Rennewald

Andrea Repele

Rogério Ribeiro

Patrick O'Neill Riley

Daniela Rimola

David Rind

Anne-Torill Rindal

Laura Rivas

Carmel Rizzotto

Bobby L. Robbins Jr.

Hanna Roberts

A. Daniel Rodriguez

Benjamin Roberto Rodriguez Obregon

Sven Roeck

Manuel Rojas

Yuliana Gabriel Romero

Brian Rose

Frederico Rosseto

Paolo Rubino

Sheila Ruscetta, USA

Betty Ryan

Jan Rytina

Martin S.

Max Sabba

Christopher Sagar

Ruqiyah Sajjad

Philippe Salierno

Diana Salsa

Irina Samarina

Cassandra Samiez

Taylor Samuelson

Nathali Loaiza Sanabria

Mason Santora

Sarawyn

Gonzalo Sarmiento

Jessica Sanchez Satarain

Emma Saunders

Gary Saxby

Ulrich Schätzlein

Karina Scheld

Conny Schict

Julian Schiller

Rachel Schins

Gino Schoeters

Tanja TJ Schulz

Chris Scully

Susanne Seidl

Carlos J. Villaplana Sequeiros

Aracely Serna

Ashley Seymour

Tomáš Shejbal

Konstantin Shkoliar

Andrew Shurmer

Tero Siltanen

Andrea Silva

David Silver

Pavel Simo

Dominika Simova

Matt Simpson

Jolanda Sinkgraven

Sirithiliel

Izzy Sissi

Miriam Skog

Lukáš Skopal

Stanislav Škorňa

Marie-Sofie Slätt

Tom Slatter

SlavaBooth

Natalia Smiech

Larey Smile

Leighton Smith

Elin (Söderblom)

Delia Soetandi

Kenneth Solberg-Harestad

Kenneth Solberg-Harestad

José María Sotomayor

Vitor Souza

Juergen Spiegl

Silje Spro

Bojana Sretenovifá

Lora Stambolova

Dr. Daniel E. Starz

László Steiner

Rebekka Stetskamp-Heinrichs

Eric Stoop

Gordon Strackbein

Tobias Straus

Barunka Stuchlikovie

Milada Stullerova

John Stutz

Holger Suhrmann

Brasitalian SunflowerS

Johanna Suominen

Ruben Suriya

Jerry W. Sutton

Marko Svagelj

Holly Sylvester

Veronika Szalay

Boglárka Szöllősi

Essi T

Cristina Taruffi

Valentina Taruffi

Patric Taylor

Rob 'WolfHeart' Taylor

Daniel Tecklenborg

Linda van Teijlingen

Maren Tenberken

Hans Thesing

Tobias Jens Thielen

Adrian Thomas

Caroline Thomas

Laura Thompson

Caith Threefires

Tiffi

Jean-Yves Tizon

Hardo Tobeck

Spencer Todaro

Ana Tomasovic

W. Tomlinson

Andru Tomoiu

Michaela Torjáková

Hope Tornowske

Shaun Towner

Andy Traeger

Chris Trapp

Harri Tuominen

Adriano Ueda & Paola Toda

Andreas Leonhart Uhlig

Laura Urban

Micky Urbany

Anna Uronen

Kimiko Ushiro

Irwan Aria Utama

Paola Valdés

Teemu Valkama

Paola Valmori

Jelma van den Brink

Veerle Van der Haar

Jamilla van Duuren

Marvin van Gessel

Peter van Hemert

Ana van Neer

Patrick Vandenbussche

Stephane Vanderreken

Ioana Varvari

Eliška Vaščáková

Tatiana Vasileva

Ariadna ♥ Vazquez

Emma Veldhuis

Lisa Vella

Petronela Vencelova

Gerbert Verheij

Cendrine Vermer

Kirsi Vestama

Marjo Viherlaakso

Henk Vinkes

Julia Virtanen

Sergio Visentin

Joe Vitoulis

Alena Vogel

Maxim Volik

Ricky Volk

Selina Voß

Rob & Cindy VW

Markus Wagner (BloodyGrin)

Nico Wallmann

Trevor Warren

Mateusz Warzycha

Ryan Webster

Thomas Webster

Kevin Weiß

Kevin Wenz

Thibaut Wetzel

Darren White

Katja Wicke

Eva Maria Wiedemann

Olga Wiering-Van Veen

Henry Wijnmalen

Arthur Williams

Karl Williams

Ariadne Willis

Mark W Wilson

Darren Winfield

Leslie Wittmann

Anna Wojtowicz

Tabitha Woodson

Dirk Wouters

Michele Wroblewski

Alan Wylie

Yatigan

Doug Yauch

In Memory of Christopher
& Michael Zack

Rafael Zaki

Ing. Veronika Zbránková

Larry Ziglar

Stephanie Zorn

Charlotte Zuercher

Еленка Дудочка

First published in the United Kingdom in 2021 by Rocket 88,
an imprint of Essential Works Limited,
40 Bowling Green Lane, London, EC1R 0NE.

Publishers: John Conway, Mal Peachey

Tarja interviews and text compiled by Natasha Scharf

Designed and set by seagulls.net

ISBN: 9781910978689

Printed by Imago in Turkey

All photos are from the personal collection of the author, except for the following:

Pages 1, 6, 16, 21 © Tony Härkönen; 2–3, 4–5, 31, 58, 127, 150 (top left), 155, 158, 162, 172, 175,
179, 184, 192, 208 © Tim Tronckoe; 7, 12, 14 © Turunen family; 9 © unknown; 11 (bottom x 6)
© Sirja Tiilikainen; 15 (bottom) © Press Photo Savonlinna Opera Festival; 17 © Press Photo Evankeliumi;
20 The Voice Finnish Official Emoji; 28, 29, 44 © Paul Harries; 51, 54–5, 135, 182 © Jens Boldt; 81
(bottom) © Jamie-David Wuestenhagen; 84 © Soledad Diez; 88, 108, 128, 129, 136, 145, 148–9
© Eugenio Mazzinghi; 94–5, 96 (top) © Ariel Pascolat; 109, 122 © Poras Chaudhary; 118 © photo
Poras Chardhary / digital art by Mikoláš Gál ; 120–1 © Alena Švambergová; 181 © Jaakko Manninen

The publisher has made every effort to contact the copyright holders of photos in this book. If there
are any omissions or errors please contact the publisher so that future editions can be amended.